Presented To:

From:

Date:

From My Heart to God

Written by Regina Brumley

ISBN 978-1-105-55056-0

Pictures from the wedding were taken by Sandy Campbell Photography of Wynnewood, OK 73057. Other photos were taken by Kellie Davis. Used by permission. All rights reserved.

Acknowledgements and Dedications

I want to thank so many people for the encouragement that they gave me in writing my blog in the beginning and developing it into this book. I am sure that if I were to start naming names of those that encouraged me I would forget some so I will simply say Thank you to EVERYONE who did so. I would like to give a special Thank You to my family Erick, Ericka, Dalton, Shanna, Cody, Addy, Aarron, Mom and Dad for being so supportive of me and dealing with my mood swings, anger, worry, and fear while I have written this. Thank you for allowing me to put a part of our lives on display in order to fulfill the calling that God has put upon my heart. I would like to extend a special Thank You to my Mom and Dad for making me the person that I am today, for giving me the understanding of just how important a close knit family is life and for always being there for me when I need you. Erick, you have been my rock through all of this. I do not know how you can grieve so deeply (and I know that you do because I have seen it) and still stand so strong when I need you. I thank God, most importantly, for giving me the calling to write this book and holding my hand along the way.

This book is dedicated to my daughter, Jessica Richelle Power. Although your life was cut way too short you taught me the importance of pushing hard for what you believe in and never giving up on it. I watched you grow from a small child with not much understanding of God to an adult who lived her life to its fullest. The difference in your life after you accepted Jesus into your heart was APPARENT to anyone who knew you. Thank You for sharing your love of Jesus with me so that I might know that it is your WISH that I trust him and lean on him through the tragedy of your loss. I will ALWAYS Love you and will hold your memory close to my heart. Smile one of those beautiful smiles for me.

Contents

Introduction

Since the death of my daughter, Jessica Power, at the young age of 18 I had become so confused and heartbroken. In my confusion I began to ask questions and feel things that I was not prepared to feel or deal with. I read some of the books out there about how to deal with the death of a child and most were focused on small children which did not fit my situation. I also found that none of them told me if what I was feeling was "normal". None of them gave me insights as to what I should expect to go through. Many told me to turn to God, which I was already doing but I needed more than that and I was having a very hard time finding that. In an effort to try and make since of everything I was urged to start a blog to write down my feelings. This was soo out of my comfort zone. I am an expert on putting on that smile and acting as if everything is fine when my world is FAR FROM IT. Opening up and allowing people to see my true feelings and flaws was a very scary thing for me to do.

In the beginning I wrote the blog in private, not sharing it with anyone. I started to feel such a feeling of KNOWING this would help others though the more that I wrote and so I sent out my link and allowed people to read what I was going through. I knew immediately that my blog was helping people from the responses that I began to get as I wrote each day. Suddenly it became apparent to me that THIS was how I could honor Jessica. THIS was how I could find some PURPOSE for her loss in my life. Once the idea of writing a book was brought up to me by people reading my blog I KNEW that this was what God wanted me to do. I am not a counselor or preacher but I feel that I am very "qualified" to write this book on grief as I have EXPERIENCED it first hand and want to be able to help people that are going through grief to make it through. My Jessica wanted more than ANYTHING to become an RN and be able to help HEAL people. She will never be able to do that in the physical aspect she WILL however, be able to help people heal emotionally through my sharing this book and how her death affected me. This book is for you Jessica. I Love and Miss you Baby.

Chapter 1

Before I was Momma

It is hard to go back and tell something that has already happened but it is important for me to explain the BEFORE in order for you to understand the after. Jessica was not originally born to me. She and her biological sister, Ericka, were born to their birth mother and their dad, Erick, who is now my husband. I have 2 children as well which were born to me and my first husband. My daughter Shanna is the oldest and my son, Dalton, is one month older than Ericka. They were all soo close in age. Shanna was born in March 1992, Jessica in May 1993, Dalton in August 1994 and Ericka in September 1994. This has only 2 years age difference between the first and 4th child so we had QUITE the chore trying to merge them all together in the beginning. There was the normal jealousy and then the confusion for Jessica and Dalton of WHERE they fit in. You see, Jessica was no longer the oldest and Dalton was no longer the baby. Sounds very simple to a grown up, but to a child this is a big deal. I will not say it was simple or quick. There were times when I thought the two families would NEVER learn to get along and that things would NEVER be normal. I will say for those of you who are trying to merge a family together it is HARD WORK but it IS possible. I would have thought it would have gotten easier when Jessica and Ericka's biological mom dropped out of the picture but in some ways it got worse. The jealousy over the fact that Shanna and Dalton still got to see their dad and that he bought them things was overwhelming and I felt for them but could do nothing to change what was. Ok, I am getting off track again so I will spare you the rest of the details about those early times and just say that we DID get through it and eventually Jessica and Ericka both came to me wanting to know what would happen to them if something were to happen to their Dad. This was the HARDEST thing for me to answer for them because you see; in all aspects that mattered to ME they were my daughters. I had been there through broken arms, lost teeth, birthday parties, first pair of glasses, and even first boyfriends (which I STILL thought they were not old enough for). But the bottom line was that I was not LEGALLY their mom and without that I did not know what would happen to them if something were to happen to him. I can still remember as if it were yesterday how my heart was so filled with emotion when, they said to me "We don't want to have to leave you. YOU are our Momma and we want to stay with you." I know that there are people who believe that it is impossible for an adopted child to be loved as much as a child that someone gave birth to but let me tell you this is NOT true. I felt as much pain and longing in that moment as I felt in all 23 1/2 hrs of labor with Shanna and Dalton. I felt the fear of losing the child that was mine just as I did when I was having trouble with the births of Shanna and Dalton. I felt the determination to keep them safe no matter what it took and I KNEW that I had to do everything in my power to keep them with me. I Love Shanna and Dalton with all of my heart but neither of them were planned pregnancies. I didn't set out to make a baby with their dad the way some couples do and then try until it happened. We simply found out one day that I was expecting despite the fact that I was on birth control and should not have been able to get pregnant. However, I wanted both of them tremendously because they were my children and I LOVED them. With Ericka and Jessica I DID set out to have them as my daughters I CHOSE to go through the court process to have their biological mother's rights taken away and to get that new birth certificate that means soo much to us all now when we see that it shows that I gave birth to both of the girls. I chose to go through all of the heartache and stress and sleepless nights of dealing with it all because I loved them with all my heart as well. From the point that Ericka and Jessica came into my life I started to love them and once they started living with us full time that love only grew and grew more and more each day. I have been in their lives since the time they were 3 and 4 and I took on the roll of Mom in their lives when they came to live with their dad and me at the ages of 5 and 6. I have tried to remember how things were before they were a part of my life and I cannot. I can remember a few moments in Shanna and Dalton's lives where I know that Ericka and Jessica were not there because of the ages that Shanna and Dalton were but somehow my memory still manages to THINK that they were. You see, I cannot remember my life without being their mom.

Chapter 2

Life AS I KNEW IT

My life was good, I had 2 beautiful daughters who had graduated High School, moved out, gotten jobs, were attending college and had just recently gotten married. My son had gotten a good job and was working full time which also took him away from home a lot more than I would like and my youngest daughter was so busy with school, work, and her social calendar that I didn't have much time with her either. This had caused me some sadness because it is so hard to not be able to see your children daily when you have been used to being able to for so long. I was beginning to learn how to deal with this though and had even started working part time again to bring in money for Christmas, which was coming up soon, and to help get our emergency funds back in shape after paying for the two weddings. My children were growing up and in just a couple of short years Erick and I would be alone. This scared me. I was not sure how I was supposed to BE with Erick alone. From day one of us being together we had children. I had been a mother almost my entire adult life. HOW was I going to deal with things once the kids moved out and on with their lives?

Oh, how I wish that was the worst I had to worry about. How I wish that my worries and heartache were only for children that I could drive to see when I felt the need to do so. I don't mean to say that these are not important feelings that I was feeling, they are. It is just that in light of what has happened since I would WELCOME those worries as they are fixable by me. Oh, how I long for the days when I had the control to fix what was wrong in my life and what affected me and those that I love.

It only takes a minute, one little occurrence, for the rug to be pulled out from under you and the life you know it to be changed to a point that it can never be as it was. It is when these things happen that you come to realize that no matter how much you THOUGHT you were in control of your life you really never were. You can control how you react to things that happen in your life and you can control decisions that you make in your life but there are some things that you just cannot change or make right no matter how much you try.

As a mother I always felt responsible for my kids. I tried to teach them respect, honesty, responsibility, good work ethics that would help them along in life. I also tried to express to them the importance of love, honesty, and commitment in a relationship. When my two oldest girls came to Erick and me only weeks apart and told us that they wanted to get married we worried. I had been married at 18 and even though I would not change getting married to him because it would have me not having the two beautiful children that came from that marriage I know that had we have been more mature at the time that we got married things would have been easier for us. I even knew that although Erick and I were older when we got together we had done a LOT of maturing and growing since getting married. So this was a worry and we expressed to both girls that we wanted them to really think about what getting married would mean. We knew that they would ultimately do what they decided should be done and we would stand behind them with whatever they decided to do but I wanted them to know that it would be hard to go to work, school, and try and keep a marriage together. This was especially a worry for me in Jessica's case because not only was SHE going to be going to school and working but so was her soon to be husband Aarron. This would make for a lot less time to spend together and a lot of working together to make things work.

Both Shanna and Jessica were both VERY SURE of the fact that they wanted to get married and spend the rest of their lives with these guys though so I began my dutiful job as mother of the bride and helped both of them to plan their weddings. Both girls were so excited and so good at planning a wedding on a limited budget. I could not have been any more proud of the young women that they had turned out to be.

November 5, 2011 was the date that Shanna and Cody were married and November 21, 2011 was the date Jessica and Aarron were married. The weddings were closely followed by Thanksgiving of course and then Christmas and New Years which had me very busy. I could not WAIT for everything to slow down in the new year of 2012 so that life could get back to normal. Little did I know that normal was far from what was in store for me and my family.

Chapter 3

My World Stood Still

January 10, 2012 started out like normal, I wasn't feeling well and running late to sub at the school which was a usual occurrence for me when I tried to do anything in the mornings. I managed to get dressed and called Jessica down at her trailer to see if she would mind to open the gate for me so I could get to school on time. She opened it for me, waved at me, and as I drove through we exchanged I love yous and I asked her if she could bring my medicine to school to me later before she went to Ardmore because I had forgotten them. As I was on my way to school I got a text from my son asking me if I was working at the school that day because he had forgotten his lunch at home and wanted me to bring it to him. This resulted in me asking Jessica if she would also mind to drop his lunch off to him on her way to Ardmore as well which she agreed to. Little did I know that when Jessica brought me my pills to the school before lunch it would be the last time I would see her sweet smiling face. I was teaching 3rd hour which happens to have my youngest daughter Ericka in it when Jessica came in and I had to listen to the two of them fuss in their sisterly manner because Jessica had not brought Ericka anything and hear Ericka BEG her to go and pick her up something. Ericka did her normal little sister pout and said that Jessica didn't love her and the three of us chuckled about that because we knew it wasn't true. Jessica was eager to get on her way because she was going to get all of her things changed over into her new last name from where she had gotten married in November and then was going to go to Chickasha to get the Tom Tom from her older sister's husband so that she and Aarron could use it to go to Louisiana that Friday to pick up their newest addition to their family. (A chocolate Pekingese puppy) So I told Jessica good bye and that I loved her and she left the room. The day seemed soo long to me and I was tired by the time last hour arrived so when Jessica texted me and asked if I wanted to ride to Chickasha with her I declined saying that I was tired and wasn't up to it. She said ok and that she would see me later that evening and that she loved me. HOW I wish I would have gone with her although I have NO IDEA if it would have made a difference in the outcome of that day or not and never will.

Some people say I am completely nuts for what I am about to say but I know that I am not. I have always bitten my fingernails from the time I was very young and I have tried MANY times to stop with no avail. However, sometime during the months of September and October while I was busy helping to plan my oldest two daughter's weddings I just stopped biting them. This should make no since at ALL because I was a nervous wreck most of the time but I did and by the time that the two of them walked down the aisle in November I had the prettiest long fingernails I had ever had. My nails continued to stay this way through Thanksgiving and Christmas and into New Years and I never tried to bite them. However, sometime a little past 4:30pm on this day I looked down and realized that I had bitten all of my fingernails off. I don't remember starting to bite them and I had no idea WHY I was biting them but I had a feeling of unease as if something was not quite right in my world and I was helpless to know why I was feeling this. Before I could ponder this any longer my phone rang and as I looked down at the caller ID I saw that it was Jessica's husband Aarron's phone. I answered figuring that it would be Jessica's voice that I heard on the other end because she was ALWAYS forgetting to charge her phone. It was not her voice that I heard however, it was Aarron's and he was crying and hysterical and my heart STOPPED! At first I could not comprehend what he was saying at all or maybe I just did not want to. Finally I understood that he was telling me that Jessica had been in a wreck. I immediately started walking down the hill to the trailer he and Jessica shared trying to tell him that it would be ok and I was on my way to get him. NO! He yelled at me, I think she is gone! I could not let myself even THINK that so I chose to ignore it. He HAD to be wrong. I am on my way to the trailer I told him and then was told that he was not there. Where was he at? He did not know. He had fallen asleep and woke up to this. He was screaming and crying and I did the unthinkable, I hung up on him. I hung up on my poor son who was hysterical! I had to think and I could not think with the sound of him in my ears. I called my husband and mechanically told him that he needed to call Aarron because Jessica had been in a wreck and Aarron was hysterical and could not tell me where she was. I then realized that my youngest daughter had taken my van to work and my truck and car were not in running condition so I called her trying to keep my voice even and said that I needed her to come home immediately and to be VERY CAREFUL and to stay calm. She wanted me to tell her why and what was wrong and I think I snapped at her that I did not have time to answer questions but I NEEDED her to do this for me. I then talked to her co-worker and explained WHY I needed her to come to me. I hung up the phone and started walking toward the end of the driveway and out onto the dead end road we lived on. I started to try and piece together where Jessica should have been off of the timeline. I called Cody to see what time Jessica had left from getting the Tom Tom from him and he told me he had not seen Jessica but that he was getting off work and would go to Shanna's work to see if she had seen her. I relayed to him that Aarron had called me and Jessica had been in a wreck and we didn't know if she had made it and to PLEASE get to Shanna for me. I don't know WHY it didn't occur to me that Aarron's car was at the trailer. This would have given me a car to take to get to the scene and also would have made me aware of the fact that Aarron must have gone WITH Jessica to Chickasha but none of these things ever hit my mind at the time. All while I am doing these things I am walking toward the direction that Ericka would be coming with the van. When she pulled up beside me I ordered her to the passenger seat and told her to put her seatbelt on and began to tell her that Jessica had been in an accident and I had to go to her.

Ericka began to sob and was saying "This is just like last time." I could not bring myself to tell her that it could be much worse than last time. You see, we had been through a wreck a little over a year before with Jessica where she had rolled her truck but she had survived with only a few bumps and bruises despite the fact that the truck was totaled. I told Ericka that we had to stay calm and that I did not know what was going on and called Erick. By this time Erick had gotten the information that Aarron had been with her in the car and had been asleep in the passenger seat and woken up AFTER the accident. (Aarron had been working nights so his sleeping made perfect since) They were taking Aarron by ambulance to the hospital and we knew nothing about Jessica yet but the wreck was between Lindsay and Maysville. (Erick has been a First Responder and Volunteer Fireman and he had kicked into that mode. Everything he said to me was in a matter of fact tone.) I hung up so I could drive and nearly lost it when I could not find the flashers on the van. Still not being able to find them I sped to the place where the accident was. As I saw the emergency lights coming nearer I told Ericka that I wanted her to stay in the van until I found out what was going on and told her NOT to get out until I came back to get her. At this point I THOUGHT I was totally in control, I would have SWORN that I knew exactly what I was doing but later I would find out that I had no idea. I remember pulling the van over behind the line of cars that were backed up from the accident and I SWORE that my husband was in his truck in front of me and I couldn't understand why he wasn't getting out and going to our daughter too. (Later I would find out that I had sped PAST him and parked on the side of the road.) My husband must have KNOWN that he needed to get there before me because when he saw me get out and start to walk toward the accident he drove past the parked cars and me. I remember walking and then running toward the accident but it seemed to take FOREVER for me to get there. All I could see was the car up ahead and I could see that the driver's side was in horrible shape. I don't remember speaking to anyone but I later found out that I did. I don't remember anything but Erick coming toward me and folding me into his arms. "Is she ok?!" I yelled at him. He looked at me with the blankest look on his face and said "She didn't make it." My world stopped!! "Where is she?! Oh God NO!!!" I could not breathe, I could not think, I could not hold myself up. I SCREAMED and I CRIED and I peed all over myself and none of that mattered. My daughter did not make it. There HAD to be some mistake! I had just seen her and had not hugged her or kissed her. My baby could NOT be gone. I was the one who was supposed to die first! They were wrong, but I looked at the car and KNEW they were not. She was still in the car and that tore me up even more. WHY were they just leaving her there?! They needed to get her out, take her to the hospital so they could try and SAVE her! I don't know if I managed to walk with Erick to the truck he sat me down in or if he carried me. I was numb and I was hurt and this could NOT be happening! I called my Dad, "Daddy, I NEED you!" It did not matter to me that I was 39 years old. I NEEDED my Daddy. I needed him to come to me and be with me and make everything better like he did when I was a child. Of course his coming did not make everything better but he came as I knew he would. I do not know how long we were at the scene, I know that my son got there and we told him she had not made it and at some point he went to the van and brought Ericka up to receive the news. Some mother I was, I had forgotten about Ericka and left her back there in the van all alone. I had left her brother, who was only a month older than her to comfort her and take care of her as I sat there like a lump just BEING. At some point during all of this I must have called Shanna or Cody, because later Shanna would tell me that I was talking calmly to her telling her to come as quickly but safely as possible and then she said I started SCREAMING HYSTERICALLY and hung up on her. Shanna knew immediately that it was BAD because she said that was not like mom. She told Cody that Mom keeps her head in things like this.

My family is wonderful! Not only did my Dad and Mom come but so did my brother and sister-in-law. They came to pick us up and hold us together so that we could go to the hospital to be with Aarron. He needed us now. He was hurting, he had lost his wife of less than 2 months and we didn't know how badly he was hurt yet either. Jessica's body had been removed from the car and was on its way to the medical examiner and then to the funeral home. There was nothing we could do for her now but I LONGED to be with her. I wanted to lie down beside her and never get up. I wanted to SCREAM and BEG God to bring her back and take me instead! But I knew the pain that I was feeling as well and I knew that I could not leave my children alone to deal with the loss of losing me either. Aarron was alright, he had been sedated because his heart rate kept going up when he would think about Jessica and would cry out "My baby is gone." He was extremely lucky physically though. He had 2 broken ribs and a punctured lung. They would keep him overnight for observation to make sure that the puncture started to heal on its own. I forced myself to stay calm as I went in to see Aarron because I knew that he needed me to. I knew that Jessica would have wanted me to so that he could stay as calm as possible. I stroked his hair and told him that we loved him and that we were here for him. I noticed that he fidgeted with his wedding ring almost constantly and had to leave the room before I lost it. It had been less than 2 months since the two of them had gotten married and now, at the age of 20 he was a widower. I went through the rest of the night on auto pilot, we ate and I don't think I ever tasted anything that went into my mouth, we took food back to the hospital for Aarron's mom and I felt panic rise inside of me when Shanna and Cody went to leave to go home to Chickasha and made them promise me they would call me as soon as they got home. I swear I did not take an easy breath until I knew they were safely there. We allowed Ericka to go spend the night at a very close friend's house and I BEGGED my 17 year old son to come and sleep with us in our bed. I just wanted everyone as close to me as I could get them. He declined my idea though and, after taking a sleeping pill I went to sleep with just Erick and me in the bed.

January 11, 2012 I awoke with an ache in my heart and immediately felt my head begin to hurt and my stomach begin to churn. SURELY it had all been a terrible dream but it wasn't. My phone rang and it was a voice from my childhood that I heard on the other end, not QUITE the same as it was more mature now but still, I remembered it and knew instantly that it was Joe, the funeral director. He was calling to let me know that they had Jessica's body there and he was willing to meet with the family any time we were ready. This could not BE.....we could not possibly be going there to pick out a casket for Jessica. She was only 18 years old; she had her whole LIFE ahead of her! Erick made the phone call to Aarron to find out if he wanted to make the arrangements or wanted us to. I could not make that call and I felt helpless as I watched the strong man I married begin to cry as he spoke to our daughter's husband and let him know that we loved him and told him that he needed to take care of HIM and we would take care of the funeral arrangements. Most of that day was a blur to me. I remember phone calls of condolences and text messages of the same and Shanna telling me that she was putting together a slide show of Jessica's life and asking if we had any pictures we wanted in it. Dalton, Erick, and I went to the salvage yard where the car was. We had to go through and get anything of hers that was left in it. No-one had thought about things like her laptop that she ALWAYS kept in her car or the CD of her and Aarron's wedding that we were sure was in there on that horrible night before. Looking at the car in the daylight was horrific. My baby had been inside that car that was in such horrible shape! Soo many questions were hitting my mind. What had happened, WHY had it happened, did she suffer? The latter was first and foremost in my mind. I did not want to think that my child had lain in that car in pain and I was not there with her. I could not handle that thought. Somehow that day I managed to coordinate a time for everyone to meet at the funeral home. We picked up Connie from the bus station on our way and made our way to the funeral home where we would all be met by my mom, dad, brother, and sister-in-law. (I should probably explain here that Erick's mom and dad were both deceased before he and I ever met. Erick was an only child TECHNICALLY but Connie had been "adopted" by his mom before she died and had been a part of the family ever since.) The drive to the funeral home to see Jessica was so hard that I do not even know how to put it into words. I wanted to remember her as that smiling, happy young woman that I had last seen but I needed to be able to see her again as well. I needed to look at her and see that she was peaceful and to tell her how much I loved her and would ALWAYS love her. I don't remember much about what was said by the funeral director at the funeral home. I know he told us about how we would see the different caskets and prices were listed, etc., etc. but none of it really sunk in. I was in a haze. I was focused on the fact that soon I would see my daughter and yet she would not be alive. I was focused on the fact that I knew that in order to do that I had to keep breathing and it seemed like such a chore to even take one breath after another. But then something that Joe had said snuck through the fog. "I am sorry Sir; I really thought they had told you. I hate to be the bearer of such bad news but she is in no condition for you to see her. You want to remember her as she was and not as she is now. I can tell you though, and I won't tell you how I know other than from experience. She did not suffer." The tears began to flow from my body and I had to stop them because we had to go down the steps and into that room where the coffins were. We had to choose which one to bury my precious child in and I KNEW that if I did not make myself be a part of that I would never forgive myself. So I went, I looked at the coffins and I did what Jessica would have wanted. I chose the least expensive and then I wept because I would not even be able to see my child lying in it. I could not get out of the funeral home soon enough. I had to leave before I fell apart. I could feel it coming on and somehow I KNEW that if I were inside that place where my child was but I could not see her when I lost it I would never make it out of there. I made it as far as outside the front door and sat on the bench in front. There I began to rock and sob. WHY had this happened?! WHY was she gone when she was such a good person and there were soo many people in this world who were NOT good and yet they still lived?! WHY could I not even SEE her?! This WAS NOT FAIR!!!! Apparently my daddy took over when I could not think. He had talked to Joe and found out what he needed from us the next day in order to actually get everything ready for the funeral and then he picked up food and took to his house to make sure we all ate. I could not think straight. I know that I ate and I know that I talked to my parents and brother that night but none of it mattered. I was on autopilot. One of my children was no longer with me and the hole inside my heart was TREMENDOUS!

January 12, 2012 There are so many things that have to be done for a funeral and you are never ready for one but when it happens unexpectedly it is so much worse. There are a million questions to ask yourself: who should the pall bearers be and how many should there be, what songs should be played, where should we have the funeral, who should we have officiate, what should we bury her in? The last may seem like it would not be important in this case because nobody was going to SEE her but it was EXTREMELY important to me. I did NOT want my child buried in torn clothes from the wreck or a sheet or whatever other horrible thoughts my mind was creating. She had to be dressed in something nice but comfortable, something that she would have wore if she were still with us. My 2 daughters were in agreement with me so this was among the things that we had to get done on this day. First on the list was to pick up the picture and frame we had ordered the night before so that it could be viewed on top of the casket. (This seemed very important since nobody was going to be able to see her.) Then we met with Joe, the funeral home director, to start planning the funeral. The place, time, and place of burial were decided and he was given the names of the pall bearers. We were to get her clothes to him later that evening and the rest of the information to him by early the next morning. Joe went over the financial responsibility of the funeral and I felt myself begin to panic. We did not HAVE almost $6000 to pay for this funeral with and, although we DID have a life insurance policy on her it had been taken out less than 2 years ago and so, in the state of Oklahoma was contestable. This meant that the insurance would go over all of her medical records for the last 6 months in order to decide if something medically could have caused the death before paying a penny. So how were we going to bury our child?! Joe was very helpful with this and gave us information on help we could get because Jessica was Choctaw Indian and then delivered the news to us that would lift the financial burden from our shoulders. My Dad and Mom, while I was rocking and sobbing outside the night before, had come to the rescue. They had told Joe that we were NOT to be burdened with the worry of this funeral, that he would pay whatever the insurance did not pay right away and that we could pay them back when the insurance paid if they ever did. I cannot explain to you how wonderful it is to have a family that is there for you when you need them. It wasn't even about the money so much, although I was soo grateful that they had offered that help. It was the knowing that they loved Jessica so much that they wanted her to have a nice burial even if they had to pay for it and that they loved me and the rest of the family enough to want to take that burden from our shoulders. It made me stop to ponder if I had shown that kind of Love to Jessica before she died. I was always trying to teach her to stand on her own feet and to take responsibility for herself and her actions. Did I also take the time to show her the love of a family? The peace of knowing that when you are down and out they are there to pick you up and dust you off? I would wonder about this for a while before deciding my answer.

The rest of the day was spent picking out the right dress for Jessica to be buried in and pictures for the slideshow along with the songs to put with it and then hurrying back home so that we could go to the funeral home with Aarron when he went there for the first time. We had found her boots in the car earlier that day and we all agreed that she should be buried with them since she had worn them CONSTANTLY since getting them except for when she was in her scrubs. Joe had given us her engagement and wedding rings that morning as well as the other things she had on her person that morning and Aarron had said that he wanted her buried with her wedding ring as well. This time in the funeral home was no easier than the last one for me. The picture of her in her wedding dress on the casket was so beautiful! She looked like a princess with her big smile, crown on her head and jewels around her neck. It was my daddy's arms I buried myself into to cry and sob about how it was not FAIR and that I wanted my daughter back! People came and brought food that night and we all tried to keep things as upbeat as possible but there was someone missing in the house and we could all feel it. By this time we knew that Aarron also would be seeing an orthopedic dr. because something was wrong with his knee and we tried to keep the conversation on him mostly and not mention Jessica because we knew we would all lose it if we did. Maybe that sounds bad to not mention the child you have lost, it isn't like we weren't all thinking of her though. In fact, I could barely think of anything ELSE but to say what I was thinking out loud would be my undoing and I KNEW this. Looking back now I am ashamed as a mother because I was no good for my other children. I know this is understandable, but for me it is unacceptable. I am a mother FIRST and I always have been. But on this day and the days before I could not be what they needed me to be. I watched as Ericka's best friend, her boy friend, and other dear friends were there for her helping her to make it through the day. I watched as Shanna and Dalton bonded together and as Erick and Dalton began to express words to each other that they had never expressed before. I could not be of much comfort to them though. I had no comfort myself. I could not tell them things would get better because I felt sure that it never would. I told them things like "Jessica would not want us to be sad" because I knew that was true and "Jessica loved you and knew that you loved her." But more than that I just could not give. I kept looking to the door that night secretly waiting for Jessica to come through the door to join us for dinner like she had soo many nights before but she did not come. My child would never walk through that door to eat with us again.

This was the picture of Jessica we sat on her casket. Thanks to Sandy Campbell Photography of Wynnewood, OK for taking these photos.

January 13, 2012 I am not a superstitious person. I don't drive the other way when I see a black cat crossing the road or worry about walking on cracks or under ladders, and I have broken enough mirrors in my time to have a MILLION years bad luck and still managed to have good years during my life. But this morning I woke up realizing it was Friday the 13th and for some reason that just added to my worry that today was going to be horrible! Looking back I am sure it had nothing at ALL to do with what day it was but I guess it was something for me to focus my mind on rather that what was ACTUALLY making the day horrible for me. Another trip to the funeral home so we could bring the last bit of what was needed for the funeral was how our day began along with visiting the flower shop to order flowers for the pall bearers to wear. My husband, bless his heart, had already taken care of the casket spray and the wreath from all of us. I could not think straight enough to make these arrangements and so I left them to him. It must have been apparent that I was only holding on by a thread because he never once complained as I left more and more for him to do, he just did them and would touch me gently every time he came near me. This touch was comforting to me; it was a sign that he loved me enough to deal with my fragility through this all. As people live their married lives they forget the importance of touch. When you first begin a romantic relationship touch is something that happens naturally, a brush of fingertips or touching knees under the table of a restaurant, holding hands, or sitting with your arms wrapped across your partner. But as the relationship goes on and you start to live your lives together LIFE gets in the way and soon you find yourself not kissing your partner each time you leave the house and touch sometimes becomes almost nonexistent. For me, at this time in my life when I realized that NONE of us are promised tomorrow that touch was soo important to me but yet was something I could not have asked for if I had tried. I NEEDED him to touch me in those gentle ways and assure me that this was not my fault and he did not blame me in any way. WHY would I be to blame? Because I was her MOTHER and mothers are supposed to keep their children safe! I remember falling apart one night during the last few days after the accident and SOBBING in the bed telling Erick that I was a terrible mother because I could not even remember what Jessica had been WEARING the day she died! He tried to explain to me that was only something you were supposed to do when they were little but I didn't CARE. I had SEEN her that day and a good mother would SURELY have noticed what she was wearing in case something was to happen! A good mother would have BEEN there when her child asked her to go with her no matter how tired she was. If I had just BEEN there I could have stopped the accident from happening! What was WRONG with me? WHY wasn't I a good enough mother to keep my baby safe?!

My Mother, wonderful woman that she is, took me to get clothes and shoes for myself so that I would have something to wear to the funeral which would be the next day. I can't even remember half of what I tried on and am soo thankful to her for being strong enough to carry on in a normal fashion when I couldn't. I thought, at the time, that I was carrying on normally but now I know that I wasn't.

Tomorrow was a dark cloud above me, one that I wanted to hurry up and pass on one hand and yet on the other I wanted it to never come. Maybe if I could just put it off God would change his mind and would bring her back. I reminded myself of how that car had looked and that if Jessica would have survived it would not have been to the kind of life that she would have wanted. Jessica had always said that she did not want to get old and be like one of the old people in the nursing home that she took care of. She had always wanted to be full of life and going and doing 101 things at a time. Living the way that she would have lived after being crushed in that car was NOT an option for her. I knew all of this and I said these things aloud. I KNEW all the right things that I was supposed to say. "She isn't suffering and is in a better place. She would have wanted us to go on with our lives." I said these things when I talked to my children and others but inside I felt ashamed. How could I KNOW all of these things and yet not be able to make myself snap out of this? How could I feel soo DESPERATE to have her back under almost ANY circumstances?

I always wonder how people with split personalities manage to live their lives. How can they go back and forth between the two people that they are inside their bodies and not go mad? I felt this worry about myself right now. Outwardly I was trying to do all the right things and say all the right things that would make everyone think I was ok and that would help everyone around me to heal. Inwardly I was dying little by little and I was angry and sad and confused and I just wanted to RAGE at the next person that said to me "I am sorry for your loss". I know that sounds hateful, all they were trying to do was let me know that they cared but each time they said those words I had no idea how to respond. Outwardly I didn't know the "proper" thing to say. "Thank you" seemed to be the only things that made any since at all but it didn't seem to be enough. Inwardly I was raging! Sorry for my loss?! Sorry that her husband is now left without a wife and her brothers and sisters can no longer hug their sister?! Sorry that I will never have grand-children from her that I can hug and watch grow up and tell stories of when their momma was young?! I didn't CARE about sorry! I wanted her BACK; I wanted all these things that were SUPPOSED to happen. She was 18 years old and her life had just started!! It was only days before that I was having trouble letting go of her enough to allow her to make her own decisions in life and now she isn't even here on EARTH!! I didn't CARE if GOD needed her up there, he could WAIT. She was MINE and I needed her MORE than God did!! (I think there is a REASON people with two personalities are not aware of the different personalities.) I was very much aware of the contradiction between what I was saying and doing and what I felt and I was about to crack.

January 14, 2012 My Mom and Dad, true to form, were waiting at the church when we got there. I saw my niece and nephew for the first time since I had lost my child and could tell they had been crying. Tears stung my eyes as I held each of them tightly and remembered only a few months earlier when we were all dancing at Jessica's wedding. My nephew, who I still thought of as a young boy was towering over me and said to me that if we needed ANYTHING to just let him know and he would come help. Where had the time gone? When had he become a young man instead of a boy? How had I missed that? I sat down with Aarron wanting to just BE THERE with him. He was all that I had left of Jessica's life as an adult now and I wanted to keep him close. I KNEW that he was hurting and I was helpless to take that pain away but I could at least BE THERE, that shoulder for him to lean on. My other children all had someone that day. Ericka had her best friend and her boyfriend, Shanna had her husband Cody, Dalton had his girlfriend Taylor, but the person Aarron had learned to lean on and had molded his whole LIFE around was not there. I felt that hole in his heart as immensely as I did the one in my own.

I don't understand what it is about death that makes the worst come out in people but it does. I am including myself in this so nobody reading this start jumping at me about throwing stones when I live in a glass house. Already though, I could feel the tension between Aarron's mom and myself. I don't know what I did to offend her other than Love her son but I could feel that I was not welcome so I pulled myself away when his family came in and watched him hurt from a distance. (Now mind you I am grieving so when I manage to pull myself together enough to THINK STRAIGHT I know that this could all be in my head. However, pulling myself together is something I cannot seem to do at this point, so I feel this hurt whether it is real or imagined.) It hurt me to do so but it was not fair to put more on him than what he already had to bear. They were his family first and so I stepped back and gave them space. After the funeral and grave side they whisked Aarron away from us along with the all of the food that was left from the funeral which was supposed to have been split between the two families. Aarron had family there to see him I was told. I took this as a message to me that we were NOT his family and I felt soo hurt. Aarron and Jessica lived on our property and had been a daily part of our lives since they got together in August. They ate 95% of their meals at my house as well as doing laundry, taking baths, and watching TV there. Now not only was my daughter gone but so was my new son, the only part of her life that was left! I understood that as a mother she was RELIEVED not to have lost her son in the accident but as a mother myself I had those SAME feelings. I stuffed these feelings DEEP inside of me though for Aarron. I would NOT make him feel more hurt and pain because of my pain. I would endure it in silence. **Let me interject here that none of this above was said to make Kim look like a bad person. This was what I FELT as a grieving Mom. Until you have BEEN a grieving mom please do not take offense to this or judge that I am feeling something that I should NOT. (For that matter, even if you HAVE been a grieving mom do not judge me until you have been ME. Everyone grieves differently and therefore they FEEL differently while they are grieving.) Whether this was because, as I perceived it, we were not welcome or for some other reason I do not know and it doesn't really MATTER. It could very easily have been that I was hurting so badly that I was angry at the WORLD and therefore took everything that people said or did**

the wrong way. The point of this is not to point fingers at who did wrong or right but to acknowledge what I FELT at the time. I FELT like I was losing what I had left of Jessica's life and it hurt. I FELT like I was alone that day without people surrounding me. I have since found out that them taking all the food was a misunderstanding and that they did not invite us to their home because they thought we had family to be with us. Although none of the things that occurred were done to hurt me I hurt none the less. (The feelings of a mourning mother sometimes make no since but they ARE what they are.)

The funeral was very well done by Steve. He talked about Jessica's life and her want to live life to its fullest and how she was so proud of getting married to Aarron and of her accomplishments of becoming a CNA and going back to college to become an RN and of Aarron for going to college. He talked about how much she loved her family and her four legged family and how as he had gotten to know Jessica it was OBVIOUS in the way that she talked about us that even when she was angry with us she loved us more than we ever knew. In that message he also gave me a bit of peace as her Mom. He told of how she loved me and was so thankful to have me in her life as her mom. This was music to my ears. I NEEDED to know that as she grew into an adult she did not regret asking me to be her Mom. She and I were both very head strong and this made for a lot of arguments. I don't think we had very many days when we didn't at least have a small spat between us. Many of them weren't even about much other than HOW to do something and within minutes one of us would apologize to the other and everything would be fine in our world again but looking back now that she was gone I had wondered if she felt that if she had been with her biological mom her life would have been better. I knew that I didn't regret one MINUTE of the life I had with her. That even through all of the sleepless nights and heartaches and tears and worry I would not have traded one single minute of it because to do so would have meant giving up that sweet child that I loved so dearly. I had no way of knowing what was in HER heart though because she was a peace maker. She always said what she thought people wanted to hear and so I had wondered, did she feel the same about me? According to Steve she did and this filled my heart with the first bit of hope I had in days. The graveside was beautiful as well. Her entire casket was covered with beautiful flowers that had been sent and the family laid the lilies on her casket that we had brought and, with heavy hearts, went back toward the family car. I quickly got into the car. I could not face these people any longer. I was hanging on by a thread and I was about to come unraveled. I was numb inside and all I wanted to do was shut down. Suddenly I looked down and realized that I was still holding Jessica's half of the heart necklace we had shared. She had purchased a heart necklace for me on mother's day a couple of years ago. Actually there were two heart necklaces that she purchased one said daughter and the other said mother. I had worn mine that said mother and had clutched hers that said daughter in my hand the entire day. I had meant to place it on her casket so that it would be buried with her. Suddenly I could not breathe. I HAD to get that necklace on the casket before they lowered it into the ground. She could NOT be put in the ground without that necklace! I scrambled out of the car and frantically told Erick that I had to put it on the casket! Together we walked back to our daughter's casket and I wept as I placed the necklace on top and returned to the car where I would wait it out until time to leave the cemetery. I don't remember much about after that. Somehow we ended up home with only the sandwiches that had been brought earlier to eat and it felt so strange for our house to be so empty. Dalton had left to take Taylor home and then went to his Dad's house for the night, Ericka had gone to Cole's house, and soon Shanna and Cody made their way back to their house in Chickasha. I am ashamed to say that I do not remember if Mikey stayed there that night with Connie and went home the next day or if he left that night. I SEEM to recall that she took him home that night. But to be honest I am not sure. My mind had simply shut down.

Below is the picture that Shanna chose to put at the end of the slideshow shown at Jessica's funeral. I believe that she did a WONDERFUL job in choosing the photo that would be the last one people would see of her on that day. When I look at her smiling face and the way she is looking back at us I believe that she is looking at us as if to say "I am going on but will wait for you in heaven."

Chapter 4

Addy and Answers

January 15, 2012 We all tried to take a little side trip from our heartbroken life today and went to visit Addy. Yes Shanna and Cody, I have to admit that this trip was not about you guys at all. I just woke up that morning with my granddaughter on my mind and KNEW that I had to see her if I had any hope of making it through another day. I called to make sure they would be home, texted Aarron to invite him to come with us and before long me, Erick, Ericka, Connie, and Aarron were on our way to Chickasha. Addy is 2 and is Cody's daughter from a previous marriage but that could not matter LESS to her Gigi and Grump. (That is the names she calls me and Erick.) She is our first grandchild and has captured both of our hearts. Her smile lights up a room and her laughter can bring a smile to the saddest of hearts. That is what we all needed today. We needed to be a part of laughter. It was even worth getting in trouble from Shanna for pouring out half of her water Shanna had told her she had to drink before she could have anything else to drink. "It is called compromise" I explained as I poured half of the water out and added tea to the cup "I am worried about her hydration." Of course she was PERFECTLY hydrated but today Gigi just needed to be able to make Addy smile and I did. :)

Our side trip from reality didn't last long though. On the way over we had talked with Aarron about whether or not he would like to talk to the truck driver who Jessica had hit. (Yes, there was a truck involved in the accident I had found out later in talking with my husband. I never saw the truck while I was at the accident. All I saw was the car. I guess I truly could only focus on where Jessica was. Nothing else seemed of any importance.) He agreed with us that he wanted to know and because a friend of ours had said she knew someone that knew the truck driver I asked her if she could find out if he was willing to meet with us. We got the call that he was willing before we left Chickasha and decided we would stop by on the way back through. This was hard for us all. This was the time we would visit, or revisit in Aarron's case, the how and whys of the accident. The driver's wife met us at the front door, invited us in and prepared us that he would cry when he talked to us. They had teenagers too which I am sure made it all the worse on him. He was very kind and answered all of the questions that were asked of him. I could not ask any questions but let Erick. I simply sat and listened in almost a haze. He was very aware of everything that had happened other than not knowing that there was a passenger in the car. (Aarron had been asleep in the passenger's seat and could not be seen.) He told us how he noticed her riding the center line when he came around the corner and was watching her but she was continuing straight, how she went a little over the line but still was continuing straight and then gradually just kept coming at him. He started to take to the right in hopes she would pull the other way and keep impact from happening but she didn't. He said that he could see her face and her eyes were open and she was smiling like she was happy about something. The whole time she was coming toward him he could see that she was happy and smiling. He went on to tell about the impact and where and how it all happened but none of that got into my brain. She was happy and smiling before she hit. She was not scared or panicked. Part of me said this could NOT be true! She was scared to DEATH of trucks, always had been, even as a passenger! Her one previous wreck had been because she saw a semi coming and was afraid he would hit her and so she overcorrected twice causing her blazer to roll. She would NOT have been smiling heading toward that truck! We had all figured in our mind that she had fallen asleep at the wheel because that was the only way we could make since of it. But he said her eyes were OPEN and she was SMILING! But then another thought began to form in my mind, one that would give me a bit of peace against the worry of my daughter suffering. Whatever the last thought was that had entered her mind before she died she was happy and smiling. She did not have that moment of fear before impact, that speeding up of the heart when you know something is about to happen and you are powerless to stop it. Aarron had told us that he remembered hearing a loud crashing noise but he never mentioned hearing Jessica scream. He would have REMEMBERED her screaming. I know this as surely as I know it requires air for us to breathe. She did not scream, she was not scared, she was happy and at peace. As we sat in this man's living room I began to think about the questions I had all my life about how and when God would take us. Suddenly I had no doubt in my mind that God had taken Jessica BEFORE she ever hit that truck. I know it makes no SINCE to believe that, but I DO. I have no DOUBT in my mind that my baby's spirit was NOT in her body when she was headed toward that truck because if it were she would NOT have been smiling. God reached down and took her spirit from her body and the act of hitting the truck was simply a way to explain her death to the world. This was comforting to me on the level that, as a mother, we want to know that our children are safe and do not suffer. However, it was maddening to me that this was PROOF that God had CHOSEN to take my child from us and that it was DELIBERATE! He didn't make a mistake; she wasn't at the wrong place at the wrong time. He KNEW he was going to take her and he didn't warn a ONE of us so we could even say goodbye!!!

Now, I KNOW that there are people who do not believe that God "takes" people. I have read John 10:10 "The thief cometh not, but for to steal, and to kill, and to destroy: I come that they might have life, and that they might have it more abundantly." I know that this means that God is saying that the thief (satan) is the one that takes life not him. I also know however, that Jessica's WORST fears were having a life as someone on drugs or a life where she would have to be "taken care of". She was a very independent person, and she had told us MANY times that she never wanted to be one of those people like she took care of in the nursing homes that could not feed themselves or take care of themselves. For HER this would have been

TORTURE. I can tell you that for her to have survived the crash that was UNDOUBTEDLY going to happen this is what she would have faced, of this I have no doubt. So when I read 1Corinthians 10:13 "There hath no temptation taken you but such as is common to man: but God *is* faithful, who will not suffer you to be tempted above that ye are able; but will with the temptation also make a way to escape, that ye may be able to bear it."

I knew that God knew, even better than me, that THIS would have been something she could not have handled. THIS is why I believe that he took her before she ever hit that truck. I KNOW that my God has the ability to save his children from suffering and I BELIEVE this is what he did. WHY he chose to do this by taking her to heaven instead of allowing the crash not to happen at all I do not know and I can't say that I am Happy with his decision but it is his and his alone and I cannot change it. I also have read Isaiah 55:8-9 "For My thoughts *are* not your thoughts, neither *are* your ways my ways, saith the Lord. For *as* the heavens are higher than the earth, so are my ways higher than your ways, and my thought than your thoughts." I KNOW this but it doesn't make it easier for me right now.

This is my precious granddaughter Addy.

Chapter 5

Left Alone

I know that a large part of why I felt so alone after Jessica's funeral was over was my own fault. I had people who wanted to call and talk to me but I just didn't FEEL like talking on the phone. It is so easy to offend someone when you are not face to face with them and even more so if it is someone that you have not been really good friends with in a while. If someone doesn't know you well enough to know that this is not something that would have bothered you BEFORE you were grieved then they tend to get upset by things that you say. I didn't have any friends who I felt really close to any more.

I had somehow become distant with the people that I used to consider a close friend. I don't even know exactly how or when it happened; I just know that it did. I have tried to look back and define when it happened but I can't really pinpoint one specific time. I know that life gets in the way and I am sure that is a lot of it but it was at this time in my life when I NEEDED someone to know me well enough to know what I needed and when I needed it that I felt the emptiness of not having that Best Friend or Friends to be there for me. I had many people who told me to call them if I needed anything but I could not call them and say "I am feeling TERRIBLE today and I need you to come sit and listen to me complain or cry or whatever." I needed that friend that I used to talk to every day that could tell from the sound of my voice if she needed to come drag me out of bed or bring a box of tissue and sit beside me. When had I lost such a precious thing? Why had I not noticed that I needed it before now? More importantly, how was I supposed to go about getting it back or building a new friendship like that when I could barely put one foot in front of the other? How could I expect to find someone who like me and WANTED to be my best friend or even a good friend when I didn't even like myself?

Erick and my kids needed me to be the kind of person who was able to keep things going and I wasn't. Of course I hadn't been for some time now because of my Lupus but Jessica's death made me even LESS of that kind of person. I WANTED to be able to keep the laundry done, house cleaned, dishes washed, and meals made but I just didn't have it in me. I tried not to complain about not getting help from the family because I didn't feel like I had any right to do so when I wasn't doing my part either. It just all seemed to be more than I could handle by myself though and the longer it went without me getting help the worse it was becoming. Not only was I emotionally distressed I could FEEL that the emotional upheaval was starting to wear on me physically as well. My Lupus was in full flare, my fibromyalgia was acting up more than it had in YEARS and now nerve issues were being added to my list of physical things that were going on with me. I was lost as to what to do and how to handle what was going on.

Chapter 6

Questioning God

January 16, 2012 I know people say you are not supposed to question God but I did. I wish I could say this was a new thing for me that I had always trusted in God to show me what to do and to handle things without questioning but I can't. I have always been impatient, I want answers NOW and when they don't come I want to know WHY they aren't coming. I also am very SURE of what I think the answers should be sometimes and very worried that I will make the wrong decision THINKING it is God when it is in fact not him giving me the answers. I don't know WHY I am that way, I just am. This has me and God having one of those relationships where he KNOWS that I will question him and he must think it is OK because he just keeps sticking with me and when I become hard headed and question him he just keeps on at me till I get it. For example: We were all living in Stratford and Ericka and Jessica had just come to live with us full time. This was something we had PRAYED would happen I had made promises to God that if he just allowed us to get them I would do right with them and would get them into church and make sure that they learned about God and Jesus. Well he did his part and I was TRYING to do mine, or at least I kept telling myself that, but I just couldn't figure out WHERE to take them. You see, I was raised Pentecostal Holiness and there aren't many of those churches around anymore. Then later in life I went to a Baptist church but there were always some things in the Baptist believes that seemed to cause me trouble and eventually SOMEONE in the congregation would find out and I would be asked to either change my beliefs or leave the church. Erick was raised Methodist but I did not UNDERSTAND their beliefs, had actually never really even been introduced to them but had heard rumors about how their beliefs were "wrong" so I just didn't know HOW I was supposed to figure out where to take them to church. I kept talking to Jesus about this, I say talking because I was a new mother of 4 and also worked 40 hours a week so praying in the normal since of the word was not something I seemed to do well. I would start out praying and end up thinking about the laundry that needed to be done or the homework that the kids needed help with or sometimes even falling asleep. This made me feel ashamed so I took to TALKING to Jesus rather than praying. I would just talk out loud to him while I was driving to or from work and I could keep focused that way. I don't know if that is the RIGHT thing to do but he didn't seem to mind. Anyway, I had been talking to him and explaining this to him and waiting for answers and becoming very impatient with him for not answering me. During this time a man would come to my kiosk where I worked many times and ask me questions about a cellular phone and how it would work in this area. He was a very nice man and I later found out in talking with him that he was the pastor of the Methodist Church in Stratford. I told my husband about this nice man and how he was always happy and kind and all the while I kept asking God when he was going to let me know where he wanted me to take the kids to church. Couldn't he just send me a SIGN? I can't remember how long I waited for this sign before one day I was waiting to pick up the kids from school in the parking lot which happens to be the Methodist Church parking lot. By this time I had found out that I was suffering from Systemic Lupus and gotten sick enough that I had to quit my job in order to have enough energy to take care of the kids. The pastor who had been stopping by my work saw me and came over to the van. His name was Charlie and he just wanted to know if I was ok. He had come by to see me and I was never there anymore. I explained to him that we had gotten custody of Erick's two children and that with them added to my two I was no longer working. I didn't mention my illness because I was still in a place where I could not talk about it. It was about this time when Ericka and Jessica came running up to me and wanted to know who this man was. I told them this was Charlie and he was the pastor of the church behind us. Ericka looked at the church questioningly and wanted to know if Charlie LIVED in there. It occurred to me at this point that she didn't even realize what a church WAS. I tried to explain it to her but it just seemed so out of her grasp. I left the parking lot ashamed that a child that I loved so much knew nothing of church and God and Jesus really. I prayed silently on the way home that God would just send me a sign SOON to show me WHERE I was supposed to take these children to church. They NEEDED to know about him. Shanna and Dalton knew what church was and knew about God and Jesus and how he gave his life for our sins but Ericka and Jessica didn't seem to and this broke my heart! We had just gotten home and were busy trying to get homework done and snacks taken care of when the doorbell rang. Who could be here? We didn't really have many visitors. I opened the door to find an older lady holding a plate of cupcakes. She said that she had noticed my children playing in the yard and wanted to bring by some cupcakes for them. She also would like to invite us to church at her church on Sunday. They were a very small congregation but they were working on their children's ministry. The church she attended was the Methodist Church. Ok God.....I get it! We started attending church that Sunday.

There were other such times for me. If something didn't fit into the mold that I had in my mind for it I would question God. Are you SURE that is what you want me to do? Each time he would just keep badgering me and sending me the "signs" I kept asking for and I would keep ignoring them until he would finally throw a rock at my head big enough that I could not miss it. This time my questioning of God wasn't about a mold that things didn't fit into though, it was about what was RIGHT and FAIR! God KNEW he was going to take my child that day and he did not even give me a GLIMPSE of that information so that I could say goodbye and then AFTER he took her I was not even allowed to SEE her and say goodbye then. HOW could he do this to me? I know I am not a model Christian, I know that I sin but I deserved more than THIS! Didn't I?! Jessica's Nana in California wanted to pay for the headstone and so we were going to look and make decisions today while all of us were still off work and could go as a group. All of this information swam through my head on this day as we went to decide what we wanted on Jessica's headstone. We all wanted the headstone as soon as possible. There was something about looking at the grave with all the flowers on it and only the little silver plaque with her name, birth and death information on it that just was unsettling. She NEEDED a headstone and so did we. But HOW do you put everything that you want remembered about someone you love on that one small piece of stone? Then there are MORE things to think of, did we get a single headstone or a double? What color of stone did we want, what size, the questions were endless and soo painful to deal with. I sat beside Aarron and saw the look of anguish cross his face as the question of single or double was asked. Placing my hand gently on his knee I said "I know you love her with all of your heart and that right now you cannot imagine EVER loving anyone else and you may NOT, but you are YOUNG. You are only 20 years old and you MIGHT so don't lock yourself into anything. Jessica would WANT you to go on with your life and if that means that someday you fall in love again and have children that is what she would want. There is a plot right beside her that is yours for as long as you want it and a headstone can be changed out and replaced if you do end up buried there and want a double". It pained me to say this. As **Jessica's** Mom I believed that my daughter was soo special, so unforgettable that Aarron could never love another. I knew that I could never love another in the way that I loved her. But as **Aarron's** Mom I knew that sometimes healing and moving forward means that you find someone else to help make it easier. I knew that nobody would EVER take Jessica's PLACE in his heart but that there MIGHT be someone out there who could make his life worth living again and that is what Jessica would have wanted, that is what I wanted for him no matter how much it might hurt me. People look at me funny when I talk about being Aarron's mom. But I am. When Aarron and Jessica got married and when Shanna and Cody got married I took both guys into my family as one of my sons. I tell them there is no -in law in the words son-in law in our family. I learned a LONG time ago that family is not made of BLOOD, it isn't about who gave BIRTH to you or who the LAW says is in your family. Family is made up of people who love and care for one another. Family is made of people who would put you above themselves to take away your pain or to help when you need it. Our immediate family had grown since November from a family of 6 to a family of 9 and was now down to a family of 8. I was not ABOUT to give up Aarron just because Jessica was gone. She was TAKEN from us and he would forever be a part of our family, even if that meant me someday accepting a new daughter and grandchildren as well. Again, I was doing what I knew was RIGHT for everyone. As I have said before, I am a mother FIRST and FOREMOST. In my mind however, I was still trying to figure out HOW to wake up each morning without Jessica's voice, without her smile, even without our daily "fights" and keep putting one foot in front of the other.

January 17, 2012 This nightmare began for me one week ago today. I thought I was fine for most of the day, I really did. Erick and Dalton went back to work today and Ericka went back to school. Mom was coming over after school to help me write thank you cards. Connie was there with me and she helped me do laundry, take care of dogs, and straighten up the house. Ericka refused to drive to school today though and so Connie was going to go and pick her up after school. She and I talked about how Ericka was going to HAVE to get back behind the wheel and Connie was going to try and get her to do that on the way home. Ericka had developed a FEAR of driving. In her mind if she got behind the wheel she might wreck too. The night before Erick had given me a list of things that needed to be done: take Tawny, our pregnant Great Dane to the vet to see about the lumps she had growing around her neck; pick up Jessica's dogs from kenneling while I was there; and go to Pauls Valley to take care of some things. I was soo exhausted that I couldn't bring myself to do them though so Connie had taken Tawny to the vet and I had told her to let them know that I would come get Jessica's dogs soon and I told Erick that I would have to wait to do the other things until tomorrow. I just hurt soo badly and felt like I had no energy left in my body. He understood and said he would see me tonight. It was after Connie had returned with Tawny and had left again to go see Ericka that I began to have this panicky feeling that I HAD to go to the cemetery. I just wanted to go for a few minutes and would be back by the time that Connie and Ericka returned but I HAD to be close to the only physical part of this earth that was left of Jessica. I had to tell her how much I Loved her and ask her to help me decide which of her dogs to keep and which ones to let go because as much as I wanted to keep them ALL I knew that I could not. I needed her to KNOW that I MISSED HER SOO MUCH!!! I just had to BE there! I drove to the cemetery and sat down in front of her grave. I let the tears rush out and I screamed and I cried and I talk and talked and talked to Jessica. I do not know what all I said to her. I remember telling her how much her brothers and sisters missed her. I told her that I wanted to do something as a memorial for her but didn't know what to do yet and asked her for guidance. I asked her to ask God to ease Aarron's pain because I was soo worried about him. I asked her to help me know which of her dogs she wanted me to keep and then I told her this had been the hardest week of my LIFE. That I had made soo many decisions that a mother should NEVER have to make and that all I really wanted right now was to be able to go back to a time when I was a child and all the decisions were made for me. I told her that I just could not make any more decisions right now, that I just needed to have someone TELL me what to do. I just wanted someone to come and tell me what to do and I would do it. It was at that moment that my Mom and Connie pulled up and my Mom came to me and said "Get up, let's get you home. We were all worried about you." It was then that I realized that I had left my phone in my car and nobody could get a hold of me. My short trip to the cemetery to visit my child had turned into 2 1/2 hours! Connie had first though that I had gone to Pauls Valley and then Mom came and Erick came home from work and people began to look for me. Erick had called ALL the kids trying to locate me and Jessica had listened to me and had sent me someone to tell me what to do.

January 18, 2012 After my mom and Connie managed to peal me from the ground yesterday, yes PEAL is the proper word here because I had somehow managed to sit at the head of Jessica's grave long enough for my entire legs to go numb, I would find out that I was sitting in a patch of stickers. I never felt a THING until Mom started to brush me off but at that point the stickers were brushed INTO my butt and I realized they were EVERYWHERE! I was cold and this is a FEAT for me. I am ALWAYS hot. In fact, the ongoing joke in my family is that I am "Mother Eskimo" and my bedroom is a walk-in freezer. At some point I had put on a jacket which again, is something I NEVER do. I still don't remember putting the coat on but I was wearing it when they found me so I must have. I was chastised by Ericka who was extremely angry at me for disappearing and scaring everyone, my mom told me to make sure I took a newspaper to sit on next time and to take my phone with me so they could find me and Erick, Shanna, and Dalton all decided that TODAY I was grounded. Connie would be my mommy sitter today and I was not to go ANYWHERE without her. Poor Connie, I think she will be soo sick of me by the time I get out of being grounded. Today I was good though and was actually home when Mom came this time to help me with the Thank You notes. People had been so gracious to us; there were so many flowers and cards sent and drinks and sandwich meat, paper plates, toilet paper, etc. But the thing that gave me the most peace through it all was the people who came and cleaned my house for me. I know that sounds crazy but you know how it is....when you are expecting company you want your house to look nice and living where we do on top of hill with no grass in our yard the floors in my house ALWAYS need to be swept because they are constantly covered with red sand. Going through the motions of everyday life for the days after Jessica's death had NOT included things like cleaning the bathroom or picking up laundry and with people coming to see us I was HORRIFIED that they would see my house like this! They came and cleaned my house while I was away picking up the dress that we would bury Jessica in and when I came home to find that it was in GREAT condition for friends and family to see it I was filled with soo much gratitude to those who had given of their time to do that for me. It has been over a week now since Jessica passed away and I am still trying to get by. Some days I do well with it and some days I just don't. I am struggling the most because Ericka is so ANGRY which I know is normal, but she takes it out on ME. I am not the only one who sees it but I am helpless to know HOW to help her. Heck, I can't even help MYSELF right now. I can tell that she is trying to shove her memories of Jessica to the back of her mind and yet I am helpless to keep her from doing it. I don't know what to do. I want to SEE Jessica's face and hear her voice and talk about her because I CAN'T let go of her memory all together but each time something is mentioned about Jessica I see that it hurts Ericka and I do not want to cause her pain. I try to talk to her about counseling but this just makes her angrier with me. PLEASE God, help her to heal because I am incapable of being what she needs me to be right now!

It hits me today that I have not bathed since Jessica died. I know, that is gross and unsanitary and I can't believe I am writing about it for people to see but I promised to be truthful in this blog and that is the truth. It wasn't that I didn't have the TIME for a bath; it was more like I DREADED taking one and I could not figure out why this was such a dreaded thing for me. I gathered up my towels and clothes and everything else I would need for my bath and went on my way to take a bath. It wasn't until I had shaved my legs, and almost finished with my bath that I realized WHY taking a bath was so dreaded for me. I mentioned before about my Lupus but I have not talked much about how it affects me. One of the biggest physical affect that it has on me is my loss of range of motion. I find it nearly impossible to wash my own back and many times I can't even get out of the bathtub without help. Jessica, being a CNA had taken over the task of washing my back for me and helping me out of bathtub. I could not even take a simple BATH without Jessica here!! HOW was I going to go on without her?! I tried to hold myself together as I called my husband into the bathroom and asked him to wash my back for me but after he left I could not keep the tears from rolling down my face. I cried, and cried, and cried until finally my sjogrens took its toll and I had no more tears to shed. My eyes were dry, my head hurt, but I was clean. Erick had changed the sheets on the bed and I let myself sink into them. Again, there was another reminder that my life was SOO entwined with Jessica's. HOW was I going to make it without her here?! WHY did I even have to ASK that question? This was not FAIR!! Suddenly it hit me, how many times over the years of my children growing up had they said to me "That isn't fair" only to have me answer them "Life isn't fair." I never knew how true those words truly were until now.

January 19, 2012 Jessica is still with me, she listens to me when I talk and even guides me when I am open enough to listen. Funny how our rolls have changed in just a little over a week. You see I was always the one listening to her and trying to guide her WHEN she was open enough to listen. As I had talked to her at her graveside Tuesday about how I could not decide which of her dogs to keep and which ones to place with someone else she listened. She listened to me explain that I would LOVE to keep Tiki because she has the sweetest personality and loves to play and is smaller so she would be easier for me to handle on my bad days but that I didn't want to keep Axel because of him being a male and marking things and I KNEW that since she had a contract of one puppy back from Tiki I would have to keep a male until she was bred. The only way I could think to keep Tiki was if she went in heat soon and I could breed her. I then explained that it would be nice to keep Livy as well because she was a liver Pekingese and I loved her coloring so much. Then, when it came to Lexi....well, we had her since she was 8 weeks old. I had told her that Aarron was keeping Dora which I knew she would be happy about and told her about how Dora KNEW Aarron was her Daddy and would go straight to him when he came over to the house. I asked her to PLEASE, just guide me in making this decision. I had missed a call from the vet who was boarding Jessica's dogs while at her graveside. The call had come just before Jessica was rescued from my endless babble to her. When I returned their call the next day I was told that Tiki had gone into heat. Jessica had guided me as to which of the dogs to keep, Tiki would stay with us.

Dealing with the dog breeding is very painful for me right now. This was something that Jessica and I did TOGETHER. Of all of the kids Jessica was the one that was always involved in the breeding aspect of it. Ericka is too social to be there when things need to be done, Dalton is a normal boy and, although he loves the dogs, would rather be doing something else than mess with them on a daily basis and Shanna doesn't live here anymore and when she did she didn't care for it anyway. Jessica always loved those puppies though and so each time I tried to really THINK about the breeding dogs it hit me like a ROCK that she would never be there to help me with another birth or to question if one of them was in heat. Soo, I have to admit that I pretty much lost it when I opened up my messages yesterday to find a message from a previous puppy buyer stating that she knew I was still in pain over my loss but she really needed her dogs AKC papers before spring and she felt like she was never going to get them. She stated "It will only be a few min. of your time and I have been very patient and as helpful as possible. So if you could find a small piece of time to just finish all this I won't bother you anymore." She went on to say that she was truly sorry for my loss and the pain I must be suffering. This was not the first message I had gotten from her about this registration since Jessica's death. I had opened my messages the day AFTER Jessica died to find a message stating that she knew my family was going through family things, but for me to please call her to get the papers done. I had responded with a quick message that said that I would call her when I was through grieving over the loss of my daughter who was only 18 at the time of her death and until then for her to please not contact me about anything. Her response was that she had not read far enough down on the posts on my fb wall to know what was going on. (Now, let me say in her behalf that this dog was born a year ago and she and I had gotten crossways over the dog and so when money was not available for me to register the dog I had not really worried about it. HOWEVER, back before Christmas she and I had begun speaking again after an apology from her and I had been working on helping her get the dog registered. This was not a SIMPLE registry though so it was taking time to go through all of the steps that were necessary to get the registration done. These steps have been finalized the first week of January but I had been substituting at the school during the day and then going to work at Papa's until 10pm at night and the AKC office is not open on weekends where we could get this finished.) However, her reasoning for needing this done NOW was that she needed the papers for the SPRING and it was JANUARY and only a little over a week since I had lost my CHILD!! Was I not FORGETTING about my child fast enough for her?! Was I taking too LONG to get my life back to normal? I was ANGRY and I was HURT and I wanted to just curl up in a little ball and tell everyone to LEAVE ME ALONE!!! Instead I wrote her this message:

I cannot believe that only 1 week after I lost my child you would be so selfish as to point out to me that it would only take a "small piece of time" to finish all of this. Right now it is taking everything that I have just to get out of bed in the morning and put one foot in front of the other. I have made decisions in the last week that no mother should EVER have to make in her life and am STILL trying to finish up everything that has to be done to finish up my daughter's finances. I cry CONSTANTLY and would literally like to just lie down and die myself at times. You mentioned needing these done by spring which is still 2 months away. Don't you think you could be a bit more understanding and back off for a bit longer? I understand that you have no idea what I am going through but for me a piece of me has been RIPPED from my body and I am not even sure how to BREATHE without that piece. Forgive me if I do not spend the few minutes of my day that I manage not to cry or scream on the phone with you and AKC. Right now I am seeing and talking to nearly NO-ONE other than family. They are the only people who are important enough to have my time right now. I am asking you again to BACK OFF and give me time to grieve over my child! Yes, I am an angry person right now. I TRY to hide it because I know that most of the time the people who get hurt from my anger are not even the ones I am angry with but sometimes I just have to let it out!

January 20, 2012 I have continually asked God WHY he would take my daughter and not even give me a chance to say goodbye. Why didn't he just give me a SIGN that that would be the last time I would see her? Since Jessica's death I have come to realize that in some ways we WERE given a gift from God. You see, generally both Ericka and I would have left to go to school before Jessica would have even gotten up. This would have meant that, since she left before we got out of school we would not have seen her at ALL that day. Dalton and Erick generally leave for work before she would have gotten out of bed as well, and with Shanna living in Chickasha there would sometimes be WEEKS in between times of them seeing each other. On the day that Jessica died however, she had seen us ALL. She had seen me and Ericka at the school, had taken Dalton's lunch to him at work and saw him there, and although he didn't get to talk to her, Erick was at the place where Dalton was working and saw her and waved at her. Then she and Aarron had gone to Chickasha where she saw Shanna. (Shanna was supposed to remember to give the Tom Tom to Cody so that they could pick it up from him but had forgotten to give it to him so they went to her work to pick it up.) Had all of the things that occurred that day not happened we would not have even SEEN her the day she died. I had to believe that God had given us that one last look at her before she died. I was forever grateful for that look BUT I was soo angry that I hadn't taken that little extra time while she was there to hug her and kiss her and say those simple little words....I Love You. I questioned God as to WHY he hadn't given me a BIGGER sign so that I would have KNOWN and done those things. Over the last few days I have come to understand WHY I could not be warned any more though. If I had known that she would die that day I would have done EVERYTHING within my power to keep her from leaving. I would have fought with everything in me against God to keep him from taking her. God saved me that battle because, no matter how hard and long I fought, he would have won. I still don't like it and I still wish there was a way to turn back time, but I KNOW that God saved me a losing battle.

Since writing this chapter I have been worried that my questioning God and not taking things as just being "right" was somehow going to cause me to be separated from Jessica forever. I even had a thought hit me once that maybe my constant questioning of God was part of what caused me to have to face this horrible tragedy. I searched to find answers to my worry about questioning God and this is what I found. There are MANY places in the Bible where people have questioned God. In Psalm 44 God was accused of falling asleep in a time of desperate need. Psalm 22 starts out "My God My God, why have you forsaken me". Jeremiah cursed the day that God created him. Nowhere in the Bible does it hide or judge people's feelings of hurt, anger, resentment or disappointment in God. Isn't a God who is soo powerful strong enough to handle our questions? Why then, have Christians along the way decided that we should not be honest with God even if it means expressing our questions? I have to say that researching this has made me feel better about how I feel. I NEEDED to know that God was not angry with me for not understanding his decisions.

Jessica and her Gorgeous smile on her wedding day.

My beautiful 3 daughter's at Jessica's wedding from left to right Ericka, Jessica, and Shanna.

My son Dalton

Me, Jessica, and her dad Erick at Jessica's wedding

My daughter Shanna and her husband Cody

Pictured above on the left is my brother Kevin and on the right is his wife Sharyne.

Pictured above is my dad, Richard, dancing with Sharyne

My granddaughter Addy

Our last complete family photo (minus Addy). Back row: Chase (my nephew), Richard (my dad), and Dalton (my son); 2nd row from the back: Kevin (my brother), Sharyne (Kevin's wife), Allison (my niece), Terry (my mom), Me, Jessica (my daughter-the bride), Aarron (Jessica's husband-the groom), and Erick (my husband-Jessica's dad); Front row: Cody (Shanna's husband), Shanna (My oldest daughter), Ericka (my youngest daughter), and Shada (Ericka's best friend and my unofficial daughter).

Jessica and her Husband Aarron on their wedding day.

To the left is a picture of my Mom, Terry.

Connie helping Jessica with her necklace at the wedding.

Mikey, Connie's son

Our Family when the kids were young.

This was made for me by another mother who lost her daughter a little while before we lost Jessica. Thank you for making this for me Tasha Myers-Moore

Chapter 7

Going Through the Motions

In the beginning here there are no specific dates because to be honest I lost track of which days what happened. I remember waking up one morning and saying to Erick "How did Connie get here"? She had been there since the day after we lost Jessica but for the LIFE of me I could not remember how she had arrived. Life was going on around me but I felt as if I was in a haze. Everyone had gone back to work and school and only Connie was left to keep me going. She did a wonderful job of it making sure that I ate, took my medication, and that the dogs were taken care of but I couldn't remember half of what I did. My brother called one day to give me a hard time about them having to check me for stickers saying that he had heard of checking people for ticks but never stickers. It was nice to hear his voice and to know that he cared enough to call and give me a hard time. There were things that had to be taken care of and they were left to me to do. Thank You Cards still had to be written and sent out; Jessica's school had to be notified of her death, all the bills that were in her name which was pretty much all of them had to be notified as well. This was all so stressful and you would THINK that people would be helpful under the circumstances but I SWEAR customer service people do not LISTEN and if they DO listen they do not care to check into anything they just want to do the MINIMUM for you. My nightmare with AT&T started when I called to explain to them that we had lost Jessica and to see about moving cell phones to other accounts. The first person I spoke to was very kind and helpful and immediately closed the cell phone account that had been Jessica's. She then had to transfer me to another department though and when that woman got on the line I explained to her that my daughter had been in a terrible accident and we had lost her. She said to me "Well, I hate to ask this, but your daughter, Jessica, she is OK right? Because I have to talk to her because you are not on this account." I was trying VERY HARD to keep myself under control but REALLY, what part of we lost her did she not understand?! NO she is not "OK" I sobbed! She DIED and you can NOT talk to her! The nightmare didn't end there but I will spare you the rest of the details because it was all too upsetting for my brain to even go back over. The short of it is that it took me 2 DAYS of being on the phone with AT&T for an HOUR each time before I was finally about to get done what I wanted done. WHY would they make this so hard on someone who has just lost a loved one? There is something REALLY wrong with this system!

I am losing weight since Jessica's death. Don't get me wrong, I NEED to lose the weight, but I am not doing anything to lose it. My jeans are getting looser and falling off of me so I KNOW I am losing. It is my nerves, I just feel on edge almost 24/7. My hands and feet go numb and my head is foggy and I am just soo tired! I am on anti-depressants but they don't make the pain go away or help you to DEAL with the hurt.

We are waiting for Jessica's Nana in California to send the check for the headstone so we can get it ordered. I really hope that the check comes soon. We need a headstone out there and we are going to put a picture of Jessica on it. This will help me I think because I will be able to see her smiling face when I go out to talk to her. I haven't gone back out there since the one week anniversary of her death when I lost track of time. I wanted to go on the 2nd week but was afraid everyone would think I was in a RUT if I did. I can FEEL when Tuesday comes though. This last week I was confused on what day it was for most of the week but when a little before 5pm hit on Tuesday my stomach went into a knot and I almost couldn't BREATH. Functioning enough to even cook dinner was not possible for me. All I could do was CRY and feel like something was being ripped from my chest again. Erick has talked to Nana since she left the funeral. She has asked how he is and how Ericka is but nothing is ever mentioned about me, Shanna, Dalton, or Aarron. That upsets me and I try not to let it but it DOES. When Jessica and Ericka were young and first started living with us on a fulltime basis I made an EFFORT to make sure that Nana had time with them. I flew to California where she lived for Thanksgiving with them ALONE so they could be with her. I did not know this woman AT ALL but didn't want Ericka and Jessica to not be able to have her in their lives. (Nana is their biological mom's mother so you can imagine that I had ALL KINDS of people telling me I was NUTS for doing this and afraid for my well being even. But I knew it was the right thing to do and so I did it.) I emailed with her over the years letting her know how things were going with them and even invited her and her husband into our home the Thanksgiving after we had gone to their place. I cannot understand WHY there is no concern for me, Shanna, Dalton, or Aarron after Jessica's death by her. Maybe it goes back to the "no blood relation" thing but that makes me soo angry to think that it is. I know our family is not the norm, Connie is introduced to everyone as my kid's aunt or Erick's sister and she is black! But she has been there as Aunt Connie since Jessica was BORN. (This REALLY gets us some looks since Erick is a pale skinned red head himself. Lol) Add to that the fact that Connie's son is named after Erick only spelled Aeryk (most of us call him Mikey) and is half black and half white. Then there is our blended family of my kids from another marriage (Shanna and Dalton) and Erick's girls and my adopted girls (Ericka and Jessica) but we ARE family regardless of whose blood runs through whose veins! I have watched Shanna and Dalton mourn the loss of their sister and can see in their eyes that they loved her just as much as they love one another. Mikey wants to get a tattoo with Jessica's name and RIP on it and Connie has lost work to be here with/for us. My mom and dad are willing to PAY for the funeral if needed because Jessica is their GRANDCHILD and they would do ANYTHING for one of their Grandchildren. And me....I have lost my daughter, it does not MATTER that I did not go through labor to give birth to her. I CHOSE to adopt her, I paid to adopt her and I have Loved her every single MINUTE that she has been with me. I have been here for all the scrapes and bruises and her ups and downs. For all of her fights with her siblings and her worries that people didn't like her. I guided her to find HER and not try to be someone else. I hugged her when she needed hugging and spanked her when she needed spanking. I laughed, cried, and even screamed with her. I was her Mom and NOBODY can take that away from me. I am PROUD to be Jessica's Mom but BECAUSE I am Jessica's mom and she is no longer with me I no longer feel whole.

January 23, 2012 Today was a rough day for me but I had a nice dinner out with the entire family tonight. It was the first night eating out with everyone since the accident. Felt a bit sad to have Jessica missing but I know she was there with us in spirit. Addy helped us all to smile and reminded us that life does still have its wonderful moments even when we are in pain. Thanks Addy, Gigi loves you sooo much!

January 27, 2012 Tomorrow is Cody's birthday and so I was supposed to get to go over and watch Addy tonight. It was truly one of those trying days though. Connie and I went to Norman to get Dalton's car worked on and I had to get my license renewed before I waited long enough that I had to retest to get it. I look like CRAP, I still have deep circles under my eyes from crying and I won't even BEGIN to try to put makeup on to cover it because I am afraid I will cry again and then it will just run everywhere. My license went out in December and somehow I didn't notice it until after Jessica's accident. Goodness knows I have no business taking the test again with my brain so scrambled right now. While we were in Norman I got a call from Shanna, she had locked her keys in her car at school. She was soo upset with herself and this isn't like her AT ALL. I can tell that she is still having a hard time dealing with Jessica's death too. I wish I knew how to make it better for her but I don't. All I can do is help her out with the key situation. Soo, Connie and I go back to Maysville so we can trade vehicles and then head to Chickasha to pick up Cody's key and on to Edmond to take it to Shanna. This has been SUCH a long day and I am soo tired. I am starting to wonder if I will be able to stay awake long enough to watch Addy tonight. I LOVE to watch her but I am just so tired and worn out emotionally. I am soo glad that Connie is here to do the driving for me. On the way back from Edmond I got a phone call from Erick that Tawny, our chocolate gene Great Dane was in labor and he had to pull a puppy. This gave me something to focus on but somehow it was bitter sweet. I had always been soo excited in the past when puppies started being born but this time Jessica was missing from the experience and it made my heart ache. We ended up taking Addy back home with us so that I could help with Tawny's labor and because she was having so much trouble and it was getting so late they agreed to let her spend the night. I believe she was my savior that night. Her sweet voice saying "I Love you Gigi" made me smile and watching her with Grump was a joy. It was a LONG night and I was tired and the sadness of Jessica not being there was JUST about to take over me when Addy walked up to the side of the whelping box, got down in front of Tawny, who was deep in the throes of a HARD and long labor, and said to her "Do you love me Momma Tawny?" As if the fact that Momma Tawny loving her would make the pain of labor disappear. For the first night since Jessica's death I slept that night. With that precious blonde headed child lying on top of me who SHOULD have made me not be able to breathe I slept peacefully.

January 29, 2012 Shanna and Cody came over today and they picked up Aarron on the way. It was so nice to have everyone here together. I miss having my family together. It was obvious that someone was missing and it made me sad, but I felt a bit of relief having everyone else here. We celebrated Cody's birthday with cake and Shanna started to clean out her old bedroom. We were making copies of the CD that Shanna had made for the funeral and wanted to make sure that they worked in the DVD player so we played them. I wanted to see it but it also brought everything home that we would never see her beautiful smiling face again other than on a CD or in a picture. We all wept and Aarron talked about how he felt like he had nothing to do. Jessica wasn't there to ask him to bring her a drink or something to eat. Oh God WHEN is this going to get easier? People say that it will get "better". WHEN is that supposed to happen? WHEN will it not hurt to talk about her or look at her photos? I have come to the conclusion that those who say it will get "better" do not mean that things will someday be ok. Things will NEVER be ok; she will never be there for another birthday, Thanksgiving, Christmas, or family picture. I just pray that someday I will be able to look back on the time that we had with her and not fall apart.

January 31, 2012 Today it has been 3 weeks that I have been without Jessica and the loss of her is still as fresh now as it was 3 weeks ago. Jessica and I went through more ups and down in our relationship together than I have with any of the other kids. After she graduated from High School and came home in 2009 we had MANY ups and downs and she wanted to be treated "as an adult" and I still saw her as a child. She and I grew a LOT together over those last two years and she became the child that I was most close to. Does that mean that I loved her more than the others? No. It means that I related to her and her life and she was with me DAILY and she became who I relied on. She and I talked, fought, and laughed together EVERY DAY. She went with me almost every time I went to town and now I find that even going to a store is a chore for me without her. I not only lost a daughter, but also a friend. I wish I had the strength to do what I know that I SHOULD and pick up and go on with my life. I cannot do that at this time though. I am going through the motions, and occasionally I have a few hours that seem ALMOST normal but then it hits me and I can barely breathe or think at times. Connie is leaving tomorrow to go back out on the truck and after that I will not have help with dinner and cleaning and the dogs. God PLEASE help me to be able to be strong enough to do what has to be done.

February 1, 2012 I put Connie on the train today to go back to work and then started back home. Home was not where I ended up though. I found myself at the cemetery, a place where I haven't been since a week after Jessica's death. Most of the flowers had blown away by now and what was left were pretty much dead. I noticed the STRANGEST thing though....the wreath that Erick had gotten for the funeral which had the streamers that said Daughter, Wife, and Sister on it seemed to still be alive. Especially the white carnations that were tipped in purple. This struck me as significant because purple was Jessica's favorite color. It was my VISUAL sign that Jessica still lived. As I looked more closely I also noticed that at the other end of the grave was an arrangement of pink tipped roses. All of the roses were dead except for one single rose. My breath literally caught in my throat when I saw this. You see, Ericka had been telling me that she missed her sister soo much and she was upset because people had told her that when they lost loved ones their loved ones would come to them and Jessica hadn't came to her. This single pink tipped rose had MEANING between Ericka and Jessica. You see, last Valentine's Day Ericka was so upset that she didn't have a valentine and Jessica had sent her roses. The roses she had sent her were this exact same rose. The fact that this rose alone was still alive was a sign that their love for one another was still alive. I stayed for about an hour this time at the cemetery and yes, I talked until I am sure Jessica was tired of hearing my voice again. I cried and told her what a hard time I was having dealing with all of this. I asked her to ask God if he would PLEASE send some healing power our way. I thanked her for the flowers as if she had sent them to us herself and then, before leaving I picked one of the purple flowers from the wreath and the pink tipped rose and brought them home and froze them. If you remember I had told Jessica the first time I visited her that I wanted to do something as a memorial of such for her and I asked her to help me to figure out what that should be. It hit me as I was driving back to the house that if knowing that I was not crazy for feeling the things that I feel about her death helps me it could also help others. THIS was what I could do to allow Jessica to still help people.

Chapter 8

Jessica's Dream

February 2, 2012 Jessica's dream was to be an RN so that she could help people to heal. She obviously was not going to be able to fulfill that dream in that way BUT I could allow her dream of healing others to still be a reality through my blog. Soo, I opened myself up to the world by posting a link to this blog that I had been writing. I had no IDEA how many people would read it and respond. Most that have read it are either thankful that it has helped them in some way or encouraging to me for writing it. Some however, have taken things that I wrote and caused trouble for myself and others and this was NOT what was meant for this blog to do. I THOUGHT, after leaving the cemetery and setting my mind on what to do to honor Jessica that I had found a bit of peace. BOY was I EVER wrong. I remember when I was younger that a Sunday school teacher once told me that when you are leading your life the way you should be and helping others is when Satan attacks the hardest. That it is THEN that he is threatened and wants to do everything he can to keep you from doing the work that would honor God. I know that this blog must be helping a lot of people because Satan has SURE attacked me HARD since I started it. He has done everything within his power to make me stop writing it and I have to say that it almost worked today. God, Keep me strong through this and if it is not in your will SHOW ME. Allow me to rest tonight and get up and start tomorrow a new because right now the want to curl up next to Jessica's grave and never get up is soo strong that I believe if I let myself stop thinking about the rest of the people that I Love soo much my body would walk there all by itself and I would do just that.

February 3, 2012 Today has been almost immobilizing for me. The stress that I have been under since starting this blog has been soo bad. I know that I should grow thicker skin in order to do this but then again I believe that my soft heart is what will allow me to help people the most. I do not like to hurt others though. I am a very selfless person and have ALWAYS put others before me so this makes it hard when I realize that I have unintentionally hurt someone. I have thought soo much and prayed over what I should do about the situation but I keep coming back to the answer that the blog NEEDS to keep going. God IS using my blog for good and I cannot take that away. Knowing this does not make it any easier for me though. I was soo upset last night over everything that I was physically sick to the point that I had to have my husband come and help me in the bathroom in the middle of the night so that I could even make it back to the bed. By morning I felt as if I had ran a 100 mile race (or at least what I THINK I would feel like if I had ran that race). My legs cramped, my neck was in soo many knots, my shoulders were stiff, my head felt as if it would explode at any moment and my heart still felt as if it had a hole in it the size of Texas. I have been told that God will not give us more than we can handle but I am SURE that God must think I am MUCH stronger than I really am. I can NOT keep going on like this. I can NOT keep feeling like this. I try and pull myself together and drag myself out of bed. Ericka is out of school today so I am looking forward to spending time with her. I have felt soo alone since Connie left out. I am alone all day long and this makes it very hard on me. I don't feel like getting out and BEING with people yet but I also don't feel like being by myself with all of my feelings all day either. I realized this morning that I have only had one bath since Jessica's death. This is a problem area for me. Asking someone to give you a bath and help you get back out of the bathtub is very humiliating. It is very hard to admit that you cannot perform one of the very basic things in life. Soo, it seems that during all of my grief and pain I have chosen to just FORGET that part of life and not deal with it. I realized today that this was not something I should do and decided I would ask Ericka to help me with a bath. Of course I had forgotten one very small detail.....Ericka is a 17 year old very social teenager. From the moment she woke up she already had her day planned out and it did not include me. She wanted to go get her paycheck and hang out with her boyfriend. I told her I needed her to help me get a bath and her answer was that I could hurry up and get one before she left. I agreed to this even though a "hurried bath" was not at all what I had in mind. On the way TO the bathroom though I got a good look around me at the house and suddenly my depression of not being able to function enough to keep the house clean hit me like a brick. I also remembered that Ericka had told her dad and me at the beginning of the week that she was going to clean her room and help me with the house on Thursday and Friday. Thursday had come and gone and she had not cleaned it and now it was Friday and she had other plans other than cleaning it today. I relayed this information to Ericka and she became upset. "But you said I could go to Cole's house." I did not handle this like an adult, I did not explain to her that I had said she could go BEFORE I remembered her words of what she was going to do and realized that she had not done them. Instead I totally lost my cool and became soo upset I LITTERALLY did not know what to do. I remember telling her to go do whatever she wanted and to heck with anything else then. (At least I THINK I used the word heck, it honestly could have been hell.) The next thing I knew I was back in my bed crying my eyes out in a fetal position and she was beside me. I just felt so alone. I felt as if I was drowning and nobody was bothering to pull me out of the water. I tried to explain to her that I just NEEDED someone. You see, Jessica was ALWAYS with me. She understood about my Systemic Lupus more than any of the other people in the family because of her medical back ground. She also understood that I was stubborn and hard headed and wouldn't ASK for help with things. So she made sure that she went with me when I went to town so that when I got anxious in the store as I sometimes did and could not remember what I came for she could help me make sure that I got what was needed and get out of the store. She was there to remind me of where I parked the car which I could NEVER seem to remember if I was in the store for more than 10 minutes. She could TELL when I was about to have a panic attack or when I was unable to think straight and drive and was there to take over for me. She also knew that it pained me more than ANYTHING to ask someone to help me with my bath so she would come to me two or three times a week and say "Let's go get your bath mom." Now I had NOBODY to do that for me and I was ashamed to ask. Jessica also made sure I remembered to take my medication which was another thing I seemed to forget if not prompted. She helped me remember what medications I needed to get refilled before I ran out of them and if one was missing she could tell me what medication it was. Nobody else in the house had any IDEA what I took on a daily basis. Who was going to help me with all of this now? I didn't want to be a burden to anyone but I simply did not know how to go on WITHOUT this help. "Why didn't you just TELL ME you wanted to spend the day with me Mom?" Ericka asked me as tears ran down her face. "Because I did not want to see the disappointment in your eyes when you had to stay home and take care of ME instead of spending time with your boyfriend." I told her. The next thing I knew Ericka was PULLING me out of bed and taking me to the bathroom where she started my bath water and helped me get into my bath. I just sat there pretty much motionless and cried as she washed my back and shaved my legs for me. I am 39 years old and my 17 year old daughter was bathing me. THIS is what all the stress, heartache, and pain have reduced me to. PLEASE LORD, help me get through this. I NEED YOU to help me, I cannot do this alone. A few hours later I would receive a message from a friend asking how I was doing and asking if there was anything she could do to help. I told her no, what else was I going to say? She did not give up though and told me that she could bring lunch or dinner over tomorrow or Sunday. I took a deep breath, swallowed my pride and told her that she didn't have to do that but dinner tomorrow would be greatly appreciated. Sometimes the little things make all the different in the world.

February 4, 2012 Somehow, after my bath yesterday, I managed to start to feel somewhat human. I have no doubt that God was holding me up and helping me walk because I know that I did not have the strength to walk on my own. I knew that he was there though. He had sent a friend to lessen the load for me tomorrow in the form of lasagna dinner and I was forever grateful to both God AND that friend that had allowed him to use her to help me. On top of that Erick had called and asked me and Ericka to meet him in Pauls Valley for lunch that day so I would not be eating lunch alone AND I would not have to figure out what to fix to eat for lunch. I could never have imagined the blessing that would come from that lunch together though. You see, Ericka had told me that SHE was driving us to Pauls Valley because I was "in NO shape to drive". This was SOO out of character for Ericka and I remember thinking that this was the way Jessica would have handled this situation. When she parked the truck at Braum's I was reminded of Jessica AGAIN as she parked the truck SOO CROOKED in the parking lot that I had to laugh and tell her to straighten it up. She laughed and said "I can't park this thing." This was the strangest thing for her to say because she was driving my truck but she GENERALLY drove the minivan! Both were the same length and size so she should have no trouble parking it. I remember right after Jessica had started driving the Expedition we had come to eat at this very place and she had parked JUST LIKE Ericka had parked today and when I had said something to her about it her response had been the same as Ericka's had just been. The only difference was that when Jessica had parked that way Dalton had been there as well and she got out of the Expedition, handed him her keys and said "Would you straighten up my truck because I can't." Lol We carried her HIGH about that for the longest time. I couldn't help but laugh as I remember this time. Ericka and I continued to sit in the truck waiting for Erick to show up so we could go in to eat. It wasn't until later on that Erick would share that when he pulled up and looked over at me in the truck and past me he saw Jessica sitting in the driver's seat of the truck as he looked at Ericka. He said he could not explain it but the way she was sitting, the way her hair was, EVERYTHING about her was Jessica. He said that he felt like he was getting to have lunch with his 3 gorgeous girls and the only thing that would have made it better would have been if Shanna and Dalton could have been there as well. My eyes filled with tears as I shared with him everything about that drive over with Ericka that seemed as if Jessica was the one with me rather than Ericka. This is crazy I KNOW because anyone who knew Ericka and Jessica would tell you that they were two VERY DIFFERENT people. They were as different as night and day. Ericka never worries about what anybody thinks of her and is very outgoing and social while Jessica worried about what EVERYONE thought of her and was very quiet and unsocial. I always teased Jessica that she was a "stick in the mud" and her Nana would tell her that she was old before her time. Jessica was always looking out for me and calling to see where I was and worrying if she couldn't find me. Ericka was always more worried about her social life and what she would miss out on if she had to stay home with me. Somehow though, on this day it was as if Jessica was here with us in Ericka's body. I had asked God SEVERAL times for just a few more minutes with Jessica. It was as if he had given that to both Erick and me on that day.

Left are Jessica and her Sister/Maid of Honor Ericka.

Nothing that I can say about today would even COMPARE to the gift that God gave us yesterday. I will say that today started out looking as if it was going to be another stressful day like yesterday, I got up to realize that the upset over my blog was still going strong and I decided that I WOULD put a stop to it RIGHT NOW. I posted to face book that I wanted everyone to leave the person they were bothering ALONE and that if this did not stop I would start deleting people from face book. This was NOT something that I wanted to do but I felt soo uplifted from yesterday that I was NOT going to let satan keep me down. Things seem to have settled since then. Erick and I managed to spend a nice day together picking up horse food and dog food and we enjoyed the lasagna our friend brought over and watched a movie together. I am not really sure our choice of movie was a smart one if we didn't want to cry though. We had wanted to see Courageous for a while but had no idea that the little girl died in a car accident. Guess that was just a LITTLE close to home for us as we both ended up bawling our eyes out in each other's arms. The best thing about today though I have left until last. You see, Erick has been very angry with God for quite a while. He had decided that there could NOT be a God because if there was he would not allow me to be sick with my Lupus and allow others to go through the pain that they go through. This had worried me and Jessica soo much. I remember after Jessica was saved she said to me once "Momma, if Dad doesn't get right with Jesus he won't get into heaven." I wasn't sure how to respond to this because I KNEW that when Erick was young he had given his life to God but I wasn't sure where that left him now that he believed that there wasn't a God. I had tried to talk to him about it several times over the last few years and each time I would just make him angry and we would end up fighting. So I had not tried in quite a while and to be honest I was scared to DEATH for him ever since Jessica had died but I could not find the strength to talk to him about it. Today, while we were in Sam's Club Erick walked to the book isle. I was talking to Shanna on the phone and didn't notice what it was that he was looking at until he picked it up and put it into the basket. Erick had put a Bible into the cart. My breath caught in my throat and I didn't DARE say anything to him for fear he would take it the wrong way and put it back. So we checked out and went home. Tonight, Erick started reading the Bible. He began at the beginning which I suppose is the right place to start. Thank you God for working in my husband's heart. PLEASE continue to work in mine. Help our family to heal and help us to use this horrible tragedy to help others as you are helping us.

February 5, 2012 I am about to go out on a HUGE limb here and talk about my life with Jesus Christ. This is big for me because I feel that I fail him MISERABLY on a daily basis. How many times have I said to someone "you are in my prayers" only to pray for them at the very moment and then not pray again all day? It isn't that I don't pray for them each time that I DO pray; it is that I forget to pray. I

LOVE my God and I know that he is an AWESOME God and I know that without him I could not make it but yet I don't remember to pray. (I am not just talking about since Jessica died either.) This is something I have struggled with my WHOLE LIFE. When I need an answer from God I go to him, of course, as you have read in my earlier postings I don't always TAKE his answers and I am working on that as well. When I am worried about something or want to thank him for something I go to God but to just go to him all day long I do not. Is that wrong? I read in the Bible that you are supposed to pray without ceasing. I get Bible verses from people throughout the day and they are OOH so comforting but if they are thinking of me enough through the day to send them to me doesn't that mean they are going to God more often than me? I don't think to pray to God to bless my food before I eat. I don't even remember to pray before I go to bed all the time. Sometimes I realize that it has been DAYS since I have prayed to God. This scares me because I am afraid that during those times of my absence from talking to God I have let him down and he is unhappy with me. By the same token, it isn't just GOD that I forget about. I forget to EAT or drink on many days until the kids or Erick come home and want dinner and then I remember that I haven't eaten or drank anything all day. (Again, this isn't something that has just started happening since Jessica's death although it HAS gotten worse since then.) I forget to do things I am supposed to do during the day on a normal basis. My Dr. tells me not to be hard on myself for this because this is a normal part of my illness (Systemic Lupus). I have memory issues and I find that my short term memory is the one that is affected the MOST by my Lupus. There are times when weeks go by and I realize that I have not called my Mom or Dad just to say Hi to them. It isn't that I do not Love them and think the WORLD of them because I DO. The days just go by so quickly and before I know it I realize that I have not called. But I also know that GOD is supposed to be the most IMPORTANT thing in my life. So HOW do I find that relationship with him where I go to him DAILY and OFTEN? Am I missing something here? Is there something WRONG with me? Am I taking the whole "praying without ceasing" thing to literally and there is some other explanation for it? I just don't know and it scares me.

I know that Jessica's death is touching many. I was contacted by an old friend today who told me she was burdened by the loss of Jessica. This is a very touchy subject for me and my family because we were all hurt by this person very much. This person not only hurt those of us who are still alive but she also hurt Jessica as well. This is not the first time that she has contacted me since we lost Jessica and I found that I needed answers so I asked for them. I don't know if I can ever get past the hurt that has been caused to me by this person but I DO KNOW that I have to try and forgive. I have read versus in the Bible that tell me I do. For instance:

"Then came Pe'-ter to him, and said, 'Lord, how often shall my brother sin against me, and I forgive him? till seven times? Jesus saith unto him, I say not unto thee, Until seven times: but, Until seventy times seven." Matthew 18:21-22.

"For if ye forgive men their trespasses, your heavenly Father will also forgive you: But if ye forgive not men their trespasses, neither will your Father forgive your trespasses." Mathew 6:14-16

"And when ye stand praying, forgive, if he have ought against any: that your Father also which is in heaven may forgive you your trespasses. But if ye do not forgive, neither will your Father which is in heaven forgive your trespasses." Mark 11:25-26

I HAVE to be forgiven by God for my sins because I HAVE to go to Heaven to see my precious Jessica again. I must admit that though I KNOW I have to forgive I have not yet. I am still seeking answers and hopefully God will continue to guide me to a point where I CAN forgive. For now I am human and I pray that if God were to take me before I reach the point of forgiveness he would forgive my inability to be as righteous as he is. I LONG to be, but I am not there yet.

Not only am I suffering pain from the loss of Jessica tonight, but for a family that I know that also lost a dear loved one. I did not know this person well, but I will always hold a dear memory of him of a date that I had to attend with him and my best friend in High School. I remember that she wanted to go out with him and her dad would not allow it unless someone went along. I remember us going out and my friend, being so worried and not knowing what to do have put me in the MIDDLE of the two of them. This would cause him to joke and laugh about how he felt like he was going out with ME instead of her. There were other things that happened that night that are clear in my mind but I will always remember him as that High School guy that joked and smiled with us. I have seen him since and to be honest, I have changed in looks so much that I don't know if he even realized who I was. He certainly never seemed to and I didn't push it. His wife is also ill and I feel for her SOO MUCH. I am having such a hard time dealing with the loss of Jessica and I am not HEATHLY, but I am not NEAR as sick as she is either. He was not just a husband, friend, family member; he was on the volunteer fire dept. here in Maysville. He was a GIVING man and many in the community knew him and will be affected by his death. I am not sure if I will make it to the funeral because it will be at the same church as Jessica's funeral and I just do not know if I can handle that. I am praying for God's guidance on that and he has not yet answered me. I have not spoken to any of the family to see if they mind me using their names in this blog so I will not do so until I have. If you are reading this though.....God KNOWS who this person is please say a prayer that he will hold the hands of their loved ones, friends, etc. and get them through the next days, weeks, months, etc. as they go on with their lives without this amazing man.

February 7. 2012 It has been 4 weeks today since Jessica died and in some ways it still feels soo unreal. I keep waiting to find that I will wake up and it will all be a terrible nightmare. I feel as if the entire world has stood still for me for the last 4 weeks on one hand and then on another had it feels as if it has been FOREVER since I have been able to see my sweet child and hold her in my arms. I miss being able to SEE her and FEEL her. I have always known that I love my children with all of my heart and that I would give my life for any of them. I had no idea just HOW MUCH I loved Jessica though until she was no longer here. The HURT that you feel when you love someone enough to give your life for them and yet were not given the chance to do so is soo excruciating! I bought yellow roses today and Erick went with me to put them on her grave. We picked up all of the dead flowers and took them away. I had to keep her grave looking nice and not leave it with dead flowers all around. She deserved to be surrounded with live flowers of lots of pretty colors not dead ones. I know that some people say that I should not go back to the cemetery on a weekly basis like this but for me it is the only place that I can feel close to her. I know she is not in that grave but she isn't here on earth with me either and so, for me that spot is where I come to talk to her and let her know that I love her and miss her.

I was asked by someone today if I thought that Jessica had ran into that truck on purpose. The thought that anyone could even THINK such a thing was maddening to me! Yes, there was a time in Jessica's life when she was a very sad girl. She had a way of feeling that she was not as "good" at things as the other kids and never really had many friends, or so she thought. All of these things had changed with her though over the last 6 months of her life. She had finally found her calling as a CNA and was going to school to become an RN. She had a job that she loved and had fallen in love with Aarron. She and I had gotten very close and she was soo excited to be married. Jessica was the happiest over the last few months that I have seen her in her entire life. Even when Jessica WAS at her lowest point in life she always worried about hurting others. (This is one of the many reasons why it was so hard to help her with when she was down or upset.) She would always worry that what she was feeling would hurt someone else and so she would say that things were fine even when they weren't. (Of course you could TELL they weren't fine because she would not have that beautiful smile on her face.) Her worry of hurting others would NEVER have allowed her to run into that truck with Aarron in the car with her because she would not have wanted to hurt him. Jessica also knew that running into a truck was no guarantee that she would die. The thing that bothered Jessica the MOST about working in the field that she did was seeing people who were alive but could not take care of themselves. She would NEVER have risked making herself or Aarron one of those people. Also, she was EXTREMELY afraid of semi trucks and had been her entire life. She would never have been able to drive toward that truck without screaming and having a HORRIFIED look on her face. She did not scream or Aarron would have heard it and the truck driver saw her SMILING! I will repeat what I have said before....I believe that Jessica's spirit was NOT in her body at the time that she hit the truck. THIS is why she was so happy; the last sight that Jessica had seen from inside her body was the heavens opening up to welcome her. Satan is REALLY trying to shake my faith and this only strengthens my knowledge that God is using me in a mighty way. There are many times that I wonder if I remembered to tell Jessica that I loved her enough or that I was proud of her. Jessica, everything I am doing I am doing for you. You made me soo proud that you found out what you wanted to do with your life to help people and you were going out and DOING it no matter how tough it was at times. I am PROUD to be able to help you continue to heal people even after your death. The last few months of your life I saw you smile more than I can remember in your entire life. I will always cherish those smiles. Thank you for sharing those with me. They help me to be unfaltering in my thinking when people ask me questions like the one I was asked today that could have caused me SUCH PAIN had I had any question at all in my mind of where you were emotionally on the day that you died. The one thing I always loved about you was your inability to hide your feelings or thoughts. Even when you tried to keep your feelings from us by SAYING what you thought we wanted to hear your true feelings and thoughts were always clearly written on your face. I thank GOD for that. You had a smile that lit up your WHOLE face and I long to see that smile again.

Chapter 9

Nothing Is Easy

February 8, 2012 Things should really be changed to make things easier on people who lose a loved one. Everything has to be so COMPLICATED. You would think that it would be understood that this would be one of the most HORRIFIC times in a person's life and so things would be made easy on them. This is FAR from the truth. First you have the LEGAL aspect of everything, the WHO is the next of kin and WHO has the authority to do what with the loved ones things. Something as simple as shutting off a phone can be SUCH a long process. I mean really, I guess NOBODY could call and shut it off and it could just keep right on being used up until the company decided to turn it off for non-payment. THEN the company would be stuck with the bill because they can't exactly get money from someone who is no longer alive! Trying to explain this to the person on the other end of the phone that is afraid they will lose their job for doing something wrong is a nightmare! Then, there is the insurance company that wants to try and make it to where nobody will even BOTHER to follow through with filing a claim so that they don't have to pay out money on it. I had NO IDEA that in the state of Oklahoma any life insurance policy that has been taken out less than 2 years from the death of someone is contestable. This means that they can try to keep from paying by digging up EVERYTHING in that person's medical files for the last 5 years!! Now I can understand this if someone dies of a medical condition but when they had a vehicle accident?! REALLY?! The laws are NOT here to protect the people but to protect the companies and it is NOT RIGHT to make people who are already hurting go through this kind of thing! I thought I had dealt with all of this and come to terms with it all and had come to the realization that there was nothing else that I could do but go through the process and wait it out. THAT was before today. The insurance company had sent us a form to fill out and in the packet there was a release of information form there that my husband filled out because he is the beneficiary on the claim. I had taken this along with the death certificate to the different offices to fill out release forms there for them to send the medical records to the insurance company so that it would speed up the process. The first place I went I had no problem with getting the records sent (or so I THOUGHT) but when I went to the other office of the same health clinic to get those records sent I was told that I could not sign the release form because I was not her next of kin, her husband is. Ok, but the policy isn't IN her husband's name it is in her dad's name. It isn't like I have a problem with Aarron having to go and sign the papers but he is having a really hard time dealing with things and I don't want to have to drag him from place to place to do it. Then you have to wonder what happens in situations where the spouse doesn't WANT to sign the release because of hard feelings. For instance....what if I had an insurance policy on me where my ex husband was the beneficiary because of our children? Now what if I died and my current husband didn't want to sign the papers because he was angry with my ex for how he had treated me or whatever. (I am NOT saying this is the situation with me because it isn't but I am trying to make a point.) Again, it seems that the laws are out to protect the WRONG person here. I can see why they would not want to release information directly TO ME. But I just needed it sent to the insurance company so we can get money to pay my dad back for the funeral expenses! THEN, to make me even MORE upset I found out that the records I THOUGHT were being sent from the other office were not being sent and nobody had bothered to tell me. They had taken my release of information form and signature along with the copy of the death certificate and said they would send them. Upon looking further AT the death certificate they realized that she was married and so just didn't send them out.) Just seems like it should be easier.

I was determined not to make this ruin my day entirely though so I left and went to the Purcell Library where I looked and found several books that I thought might be helpful to me and my family to do with dealing with grief. I went to the front to fill out for a library card so I could check out the books only to be told that I could not GET one because I did not live in McClain company because it is a County ran library and only people who live, work, or go to school in the county can use the library. Guess the fact that my tax dollars that I spend in their Wal-Mart and Tractor Supply store doesn't count for anything!

I talked to someone about Jessica's death and the things that happened that day and after for the first time today. I have written about it in the past but not spoken to anyone about it face to face. I am sure she thought I was very heartless because I hardly cried as I talked about it. I am not heartless, my eyes have cried soo many tears that I think they have dried up. I am to the point of almost being numb now. No tears that I shed will bring back my baby. Keeping it inside and not talking about it has not done me any good. I have hid out from people afraid that if I spoke and cried I would make them uncomfortable and afraid that if I spoke and DIDN'T cry I would be thought of as not mourning her. Today I spoke about it, about HER without worry of what anyone thought of me. I cannot change what people think or say anyway. I cannot change what I feel or how I relate to it. I am Jessica's Mom and some days I cry, some days I laugh, some days I scream, and some days I do a bit of all of them. But today I know that Jessica was smiling down on me as she saw me put aside my fear of going out and going out for the first time since she died ALONE. One small step but such a GIANT achievement. Thank you Jessica, I Love You and Miss you GREATLY.

Psalm 34:18
The Lord *is* nigh unto them that are of a broken heart; and saveth such as be of a contrite spirit.

February 9, 2012 Today has been the first DECENT day that I have had since Jessica passed away. Didn't say it was good, just bearable. Downfalls were that I found that Maysville library has NO books on dealing with grief which I find a terrible loss for those who need them and the Pauls Valley library has 3 and will only let you check out one at a time because if you check out all of them others won't have any if they need them. Guess there are good AND bad things about living in a small town. Other than that though I managed to make it through the day without any more setbacks in my mood. (I say this because my mood is like a WHIRLWIND these last few weeks.) Dad called me with some good news which was great to hear and my medicine seems to be helping with my neurological issues (I think I mentioned before that I had to go to the Dr. and get new meds because my Lupus is in full swing again.) and so I was actually able to get a good night's sleep for once.

I talked with a friend today who lost a child many years ago and he really gave me some things to think about. He reminded me that our children, no matter how much we think of them as OURS, are not really ours at all. He reminded me that our children belong to GOD and he only allows us to have them for a time. I have been so ANGRY and selfish wanting to know WHY God took Jessica, my CHILD from me so soon. I never stopped to think that she was HIS child. He never had to give her to me AT ALL. He never had to share her with me. What a blessing I had from him that he DID give her to me. What blessings I have for being able to live her life with her and have all of the wonderful memories that we shared. (This doesn't stop me from hurting and it doesn't stop me from wishing that I had more time with her but it DOES help me to be a little less angry at God.) He also said to me that when he lost his son he began to have a much better understanding of the Love that God had for him. He pointed out that he could NEVER give his child for his life, little on the life of sinners and people who do not live their lives right yet God gave his son for all the sinners in the world. I thought about this and he was right. I would have given MY LIFE for the life of my child in an INSTANT, but if someone were to tell me that I could live if I just allowed my child to suffer and die I would have declined without second thought. And if the thought was even MENTIONED that I give my child's life for the life of sinners I would have died ribbing the eyes out of the person who suggested such a thing. My children are my LIFE and I would not have enough love in my heart to give their lives to save a million others. God did though. God watched from above as his son was tortured beyond belief and DIED on the cross for all sinners then and to come. And what is amazing to me is that even as Jesus hung from that cross dying he said to God

"Forgive them father for they know not what they do." What FAITH and UNDERSTANDING Jesus had. I want an understanding and a love like that. I admit that I am FAR from it but I want it and I PRAY that God will help me to achieve it because at times like now, when I am hurting soo much that there seems to be no comfort or understanding for what I am going through I KNOW that this is what will see me through.

February 10, 2012 It has been 1 month today since Jessica died. I wish I could say that I am better and that I have learned to cope well but I have not. I still cry, become angry, and lose my will to even TRY. I look at pictures of Jessica and listen to voicemails I have saved on my phone from her and sometimes I even manage to do so without tears in my eyes. I can also tell you though that every minute of every day I grieve over the loss of her. I LONG to feel her touch and to be able to see her in some way other than on a page of paper or a TV screen. There are even times when part of me wants to help time along for me to go to heaven and see her but I KNOW this is not the answer. I KNOW that it is not what she would want me to and more importantly it is not what GOD would want me to do so I somehow, with God's help, push forward.

Today I wanted to give my sweet child something special. I know that she is not in the grave where her body lies but I still believe that she can SEE it. I believe that when I bring something there she looks down from above and smiles at me or shakes her head at me when I do something silly. So, it was important that what I brought to her was just what I wanted it to be. I could not find what I wanted, I had a very certain thing that I was looking for, and so I decided to make it myself. First off it had to have purple flowers in it. These were Jessica's favorite color so this was a MUST. Secondly it had to have at least one Lilly in it because this was her favorite flower. Thirdly it had to have something Tweety Bird on it because Jessica was CRAZY About Tweety Bird. Fourthly I wanted it to say something meaningful, some message from me to her that would show how much we still care for her. I accomplished this by writing the words: Always in Our Hearts on the container that held the flowers and attaching a Tweety Bird Key Chain (the only thing Tweety I could find). I have to say that the end results were PERFECT! When I showed Aarron the pictures of it he said that it was "Jess in soo many ways" and I have to agree with him. I know that she looked down on it and was proud to have been given it. I made sure to put stakes into the ground from it to keep it in place because today was such a windy day. I hope that it will still be there the next time I go to see her but if it isn't I at least know she got to enjoy it today.

I wish that I could say that this made my day a good one but I can't. The knowledge that today was the month anniversary of her death loomed over me and the rest of the family like a dark cloud. At some point during the day both Ericka and Dalton cried over the loss of a sister that they miss so much and again, I was helpless to take their pain away. I also had spent a great part of the day crying and trying to convince myself that today was "just another day" and that the fact that it was one month didn't really mean anything. That is UNTIL Ericka and I drove to Lindsay and drove up on a wreck. The wreck was between a semi truck and a pickup truck and it made the blood in my veins literally FREEZE! I could feel my heart pounding so hard it could pound right out of my chest as I noticed that someone was on the ground outside of the trucks. I only managed to breathe a SLIGHT sigh of relief when I noticed that the person was moving. Even after that I felt a shiver run down my spine as the ambulance, fire truck, and other rescue vehicles sped past us with their lights and sirens going. Outwardly I did my BEST to hold myself together because Ericka was driving and I KNEW I could not afford to give into the panic that was soo close to bubbling over the surface but inside I was FRANTIC. HOW could this be happening to someone else? HOW could this be happening literally ONE MONTH from Jessica's accident?! I know that God was holding my hand because I DID manage to pretend to be calm for Ericka and we DID manage to make it to Lindsay and back safely. I thank GOD for being there for me and not letting me completely fall apart.

These are pictures of the gift that I made for Jessica on the one month anniversary of her death. HOW I wish they were in color so you could see the beautiful purple flowers.

Many people have tried to be of help to our family during the last month and most of them HAVE helped in some way. There are ALWAYS those that seem to say things that just make NO SINCE though and I find myself wondering WHY they would say such a thing to someone who is so obviously hurting! For instance: God does not take people Satan does. How OBSURD is that?! In the Bible God took MANY people when he sent the great flood. He also took lives when he commanded Israel to kill the Canaanites. So HOW can someone say that God does not take people? Also, I serve a God who has mercy and so I cannot FATHAM that even IF Satan was somehow involved in Jessica's death that God would not have taken her before she had the chance to suffer from such a horrible death. To say that Satan is responsible for deaths ALWAYS is unconceivable to me and to be quite honest would not give me comfort in ANY WAY. Even IF Satan was responsible for the accident that took Jessica's life I KNOW that God was the one that took Jessica to heaven so he STILL took her to heaven. If SATAN would have taken her she would have gone to HELL because Satan is not ALLOWED in heaven, he has been cast out! The other thing I hear a lot is that knowing scriptures will not help you, that you have to live your life DAILY with FAITH in God. Yes, I DO believe that God wishes for us to go to him daily and with the faith of a child. But scriptures are what give us comfort in our time of need. The Bible is what God gave us to LEARN from and therefore the scriptures are what we BUILD our faith on. I have always been one who said "God helps those who help themselves" and I still believe this to be true but I also know that God does not give us more than we can bare and soo, there are times when we are at our lowest that God KNOWS we cannot help ourselves and it is during those times that he carries us.

February 11, 2012 I have spent a lot of time trying to find a way through this haze that I am in and a lot of the help that I get comes from reading books and talking with others that have been through situations like I have. Most of what I get from others is generally helpful but I am soo surprised to read some of the things that are said in the books that I read. In one book that I read the woman, who had lost her husband, flat out said that she did not believe in God but did believe that her husband was in a better place. Now I must admit that I read this ENTIRE book trying to find out HOW she felt that he was in a better place if there wasn't a God. I finished this book more confused than I was when I started it and wondering HOW this woman was being able to go on from day to day without the presence of God in her life to help her to get through. I know that I do not probably pray as much or as WELL as I should but I KNOW that it is GOD that gets me through each day. It is HIM that I cried to last night almost uncontrollably when I was so worried about another one of my children. It was HIM that I asked my husband to pray WITH me to that God would give my child the strength to carry on and to accept what could not be changed. It was GOD that I pleaded with in this prayer saying that I could NOT handle losing another child.

In another book that I read I had been able to relate with almost all of the things that the person who had written the book had said and felt. She talked about feeling full of despair and of needing people but not being able to ASK for the help that was needed because you are soo far down in that hole of despair that you can't even seem to lift your arm to reach for the phone and call. But toward the end of the book there was a list of things that was labeled as "Things you should not say to someone who has lost a child". Most of the things on the list I agreed with because I had heard them several times myself and knew that they had not brought me any comfort and sometimes even brought me sorrow. Things like "At least you had her for 18 years" or "But you have other children; some people who lose their child don't have any others". I could even add a few of my own seeing how Jessica was not my biological child and most people around here knew that. Things like "well at least it wasn't your 'real' child that you lost". (I guess because I did not give BIRTH to her this made her a "FAKE CHILD"?! But one of the things that were on the list in this book of things NOT to say to someone who had lost a child was "Children belong to God and he only allows us to borrow them for a while". Now while this is not a statement in ITSELF that would bring me much comfort because I am quite selfish right now and can't seem to understand why God, who will have the REST OF ETERNITY with Jessica couldn't just allow me to "borrow" her for a while longer it DID help to give me a bit of understanding as to JUST HOW MUCH God Loved me. He GAVE me this wonderful child to Love, enjoy, nurture, and share with the world when he could have given her to someone else or even kept her all for himself. We are very well aware of the fact that God gave his only begotten Son, Jesus, to die on the cross for our sins but we seem to overlook the fact that God has had MANY sons and daughters since then that he has given to those of us who have been lucky enough to be moms and dads. When I think of my life without my children, without the JOYS and even the HEARTACHES that they have brought to my life I am soo thankful that God blessed me with them. I believe that although it might not be the thing that we WANT to hear during the loss of our child it is certainly something that we NEED to know so that we can trust God enough to help us to heal. Also, I think that the best thing for people to know when trying to figure out what to say to someone that has lost a child is that sometimes there just is NOT a right thing to say. Understand when talking to someone who has lost a child that they are RAW; they feel as if their entire nerve endings and feelings are suddenly on the OUTSIDE rather than the inside. They don't MEAN to become angry over stupid little things but they DO. They don't mean to take it personally if you don't call or go by to see them but they DO. It is hard enough as humans to function in the way that we should when we are completely in control and when someone loses a child they are ANYTHING but in control. I cannot honestly tell you WHO is in control of my body sometimes. I do and say things that I later am ashamed of or at least think "why didn't I think about that more"? So for those friends and loved ones of a grieving parent REMEMBER that the things they say are said out of pain and give those words to GOD to guide you on how to react to them. Remember that your friend or loved one needs you more now than they have probably EVER needed you in their lives and yet they don't have the STRENGTH to ask for it themselves.

February 12, 2012 I got to see the family again. Not all of them together unfortunately because Mom and Dad were not able to come as we had hoped that they would but Erick and I did go and see them last night so that helped. Aarron, Shanna, Cody, and Addy all came out to the house and it was so great to have them all there. I always feel the empty space in my life where Jessica should be but the space feels a little less empty when we all get together. I can see a little bit of her in each of them and this helps as well. It is funny how we all have characteristics that are just soo Jessica and yet we really never noticed them when she was alive. Dalton was talking about how he had eaten a lot and was still hungry and Aarron laughed saying that he sounded like Jessica who was hungry and wanted to eat every 2 hours. Lol Addy walking around with her little blonde head and blue eyes and smiling that smile that can light up the whole room reminds me of how Jessica looked when she was younger and still looked when she was happy. We all ate stew for dinner thanks to my Mom who had sent it home with me last night. Stew was one of Jessica's favorite things that I cooked and it has always been Shanna's as well. It never dawned on me that the two of them had this in common until today. Even the grilled cheese that I made for Addy and the people in the house that didn't like stew was something that Jessica could have eaten her WEIGHT in. She was not with us physically today but she was EVERYWHERE in that house and, with the help of my other children and my husband here with me, I was able to handle it without feeling completely debilitated. Thank God for small favors and great family.

February 13, 2012 Today was one of those days where my body and mind just wouldn't seem to wake up. I woke up this morning enough to know that Dalton was taking Ericka to school and that he was not working today because of the weather and then I fell back asleep. I just felt so TIRED. My joints hurt from the cold outside (it had snowed overnight) and I simply wanted to stay in bed until it hurt less to move. I vaguely remember Shanna giving me a call to find out information about school and me telling her that I would look when I got up but even that conversation was a haze to me. The next thing I remember I got a text from Shanna asking me to please call her and upon looking at the clock I realized that it was 2pm. I was worried about Dalton because he had asked me if I would go to Pauls Valley with him later and I couldn't hear him in the house but found that he had been asleep the whole time as well. WHEN is it going to get easier?

When am I going to have the strength to clean the house and do the laundry without it feeling like it is a HUGE undertaking?! I feel so drained and so overwhelmed!

I have been working on everyone's taxes in our house and this has been a struggle for me as well. To type in Jessica's name and information and to SEE how hard she worked last year and what she accomplished in that ONE YEAR and to know that I cannot tell her how proud I am of her and that she will not be able to share any of the return from it with Aarron. I find myself sobbing again and I wonder when little things are going to stop making me cry like this as well. It hurts so much to think of her. Just then a song hit my mind though.....it is an old song sung by Ronnie Milsap. The words say "I wouldn't have missed it for the world. Wouldn't have missed loving you girl. You make my whole life worthwhile, with your smile. I wouldn't trade one memory cus it means too much to me. Even though I lost you girl, I wouldn't have missed it for the world." I realize that this song is soo true. The memories hurt but I wouldn't trade any of them for the WORLD! The memories are all I have left of Jessica now and even when they make me cry I still cherish each and every one of them.

February 14, 2012 Today I awoke with a purpose in my heart. Today was Valentine's Day and I had a feeling inside my heart that I needed to make Jessica's presence known to those that loved her so much. Each of her siblings, her dad, and her husband would receive a final Valentine's Day gift from Jessica through me. I knew this was what I was being led to do but I had no idea WHAT I was going to get them except for Ericka. Ericka's gift was very clear to me from the moment that I woke up. A single pink tipped rose was what I was after to give to her from Jessica because these were the roses that she had sent to her last year on Valentine's Day. I was not sure what to get for the others as I made my way to the Wal-Mart but I knew that I would know it when I saw it. When I arrived at Wal-Mart I found the rose easily but was starting to feel pretty down because the ENTIRE ISLE of Valentine's things was almost empty. As I was about to fall into despair a woman came up and hugged me. This woman is from Maysville and I know her and her family but we have never been really "friends" but I know that she is a Christian woman and I think a lot of her and her family. I can't remember exactly what she said to me but it was something to the effect of "I am not even going to ask how you are. I just want you to know that I am praying for you and you will make it through this." It was soo wonderful to have someone just hug you and let you know that they are there but not expect you to answer questions or talk. I knew at that moment that God was sending me the courage through her hug to keep looking for that special gift. At the other end of the store I found it.

The perfect gift from Jessica, a rose that could have a recorded message put on it and I knew EXACTLY what Jessica would want to say to them. You see when Jessica would call and leave a voicemail for any of us on her phone you could always tell if you were "in trouble" with her or she was upset with you or not by the way she ended the voicemail. If you hear the words "I Love You, Bye" then you knew that all was right. These were the words that I recorded onto each rose from a voicemail that I had saved from Jessica on my phone. This was Jessica's way of telling each of them that she loved them and that everything was alright and it also allowed her to be able to say good bye to each of them as I knew that she wanted to do so badly. I finished my shopping trip by purchasing a purple Valentine's Day balloon for Jessica and then went home and recorded the message onto each of the roses and waited to give them to them. Of course the roses brought tears to everyone's eyes and for a brief moment I was afraid that I had caused them more pain which I did not want to do. But I know that this will be something they will cherish for years to come. A way they can hear Jessica's voice telling them that she Loves them when they need that and I KNEW that this was what she would have wanted to do if she were able to do it for them herself.

Valentine Roses with Jessica's recorded message.

Ericka and I went to the cemetery to take the card Ericka had gotten and the balloon that I had gotten and put them on Jessica's grave. As we arrived I noticed that Dalton had already been there that morning. I knew this because the day before he had purchased a wooden carving with two crosses and a heart in the middle of it and it had been placed on Jessica's grave. I spoke to Jessica again and told her how much I missed her and loved her and tears began to flow down my face. Ericka urged me toward the car saying that she had to go to work and I was feeling a bit angry at her because I did not want to leave yet. I wanted to stay and spend a bit more time with Jessica but could tell that she was not up to it. When we went to leave the cemetery I noticed that there was a small "garden" of sorts at one of the graves behind the headstone and I drove to it so that I could see it better. As I went to back up so that I could leave my normal way Ericka said "Mom, you know you can drive straight and get out of here right?" She was right I realized so I continued forward and just as I was about to make the turn to leave out I looked to my right and noticed a tall headstone that was in the shape of an arrow. This was a very odd thing and so it caught my attention. What I read on the headstone was even MORE amazing to me though. On the headstone were the words:

Do not stand at my grave and weep,

I am not there; I do not sleep.

I am a thousand winds that blow,

I am the diamond glints of snow,

I am the sun on ripened grain,

I am the gentle autumn rain.

When you awaken in the morning's hush

I am the swift uplifting rush

Of quiet birds in circling flight.

I am the soft star-shine at night.

Do not stand at my grave and cry,

I am not there; I did not die.

This was the poem that we had chosen to put on the programs for Jessica's funeral. I had been to that cemetery countless times and NEVER noticed this. As I pointed it out to Ericka she said to me "Momma, that is a message from Jessica, you know that don't you"? I knew she was right. My sweet daughter was telling me it was ok for me not to stand at her grave and cry for longer that day.

It was a late night of talking about Jessica and what we remembered about her and the things that we cherished about her as well as talking about how we had all come to be a family. We talked about how we were all dealing with her loss and how some days we ALMOST feel normal but that even then she is CONSTANTLY on our minds. We talked about how there were times when we felt like we were being CRUSHED from the weight of it all and we had to force ourselves to even breathe or put one foot in front of the other. There were times that we cried; times that we laughed and sometimes we didn't even know WHAT emotion to show as we talked to one another. We just allowed each other to BE THERE and to say, think, or feel whatever we needed to. This is the most comforting thing that you can do for each other when you lose someone so close to your heart. We live in a "fix it" world. We want to fix everyone's problems and make them better. We don't want to watch someone cry or hurt because it hurts us. But death is not something that can be fixed. It is something that REQUIRES that you cry and hurt in order to be able to heal. This is something we all understood and allowed one another the freedom to do this without judgment or being condemned. I learned soo much about the KIND of Love that Aarron had for Jessica during our talks last night. I could always tell that they loved one another DEEPLY but in listening to him talk I TRUELY know that she was a LUCKY LADY to have someone that Loved her soo deeply and so completely! His happiness was in HER happiness. He would have done ANYTHING for her because it would make her happy and because SHE was happy so was he. How many of us can say that we live our lives making our husband/wife happy because there happiness IS our happiness? He told me that this was how he was making it now, that he was going to continue to live his life the way Jessica would want him to. At first this worried me to hear him say this. I didn't want him to live his life for Jessica I wanted him to live his life for HIM. But then it hit me, his happiness IS in what Jessica wants for him. She is his guide now, his beacon in the darkness that keeps him on a path to a life that will be fulfilling and pleasing to God. It amazes me how much they had in only a few short months and it ANGERS me that their love was cut so short. It isn't FAIR and I HATE it but I cannot change it. What I do know is that I want a Love like that for each of my kids. It was nearing 3 am when we got Aarron home and I worried about Erick being able to get up and go to work the next morning. I had an ease about me though as far as Aarron was concerned. He is SUCH a strong young man and is soo grounded in his faith of God that he WILL make it through this. It will be HARD and sometimes will even seem IMPOSSIBLE for him to bare the grief that he feels in his heart but he will make it through. I lay in the bed and couldn't sleep for a while thinking about how BLESSED the two of them had been and how the loss of Jessica had changed soo much in our lives. For us the result of Jessica's death is so bleak and negative but I PRAY that some day we will be able to see the positive impact that it has had on others. I KNOW that no matter what the positive will NEVER be worth the loss of Jessica to us but I know that it would make Jessica smile to know that she had impacted someone's life in a good way and it would make my day to know that she was smiling down on us.

February 15, 2012 Today has been one of those days for me physically. I can't put my finger on exactly WHAT it is that is wrong I just don't feel well. For anyone who has never experienced something like Lupus on a daily basis this probably sounds strange I know. My joints hurt, my muscles ache, my strength feels completely GONE, but these are all normal things that I feel on a daily basis so none of them would explain the feeling that I just feel less "well" than I generally do. I didn't make it to sleep until about 5am last night so I thought I had done fairly well when I managed to drag myself out of bed by around noon. (Of course this was AFTER I had taken a call from Dalton around 8am and then one from Shanna and one from Erick around 10 this morning while I was still in bed that apparently I was NOT completely awake for.) I FORCED myself to eat a ham and cheese hot pocket and eat some chips because I really did not feel like eating at all, took my daily medication and then just felt like I felt soo incredibly warn out. I can't honestly tell you WHAT I did from then until a little after 3:15pm when Ericka came home. By the time she got here I was feeling clammy and weak and was sweating like it was 100 degrees which I KNOW it was not. She and I talked a little and then she left at a little after 4pm to go and look at a possible prom dress. I managed to motivate myself enough to work on my blog a little even adding a music page with songs on it that have a special place in my heart where Jessica is concerned and when Erick came home from work he and I managed to cook bacon and eggs together for dinner. Erick, Dalton, and I all ate together and by this time I was just EXHAUSTED and was still having the sweats, and now also had added a feeling of unease in my stomach. Not like an upset stomach, just not easy. By a little after 7 pm I kissed Erick good night and went to bed. I wish I had more to say about today. I wish I had words of wisdom or a better understanding of what is going on with me but I don't. I am supposed to take Aarron to sign papers for medical record releases tomorrow and then go with Shanna and Cody to look at a house. God PLEASE help me to shake loose from whatever it is that is causing me to feel this way. I know that even when I have no idea what is going on with me you do and you can help me to overcome it.

February 16, 2012 Today my worry was not for me and how I was feeling since losing Jessica. My concern was for others who are suffering. I found out from someone who cares about Ericka a lot that she has been trying to "deal" with Jessica's death by convincing herself that Jessica is away on a long vacation. I understand her want to keep from hurting but I KNOW this is not healthy. I have no idea how to get through to her though. I TRIED to explain my worries to her and she didn't seem to get why this was a bad thing for her to do. I should have been prepared for this because this is how Ericka has handled all bad things in her life. She pushes them to the back of her mind and "forgets" about them so that they do not hurt her. I can NOT allow her to forget her sister though. Number one, I know that Ericka will not ever be TRUELY able to forget her and this will cause her to become angrier with Jessica each day that she doesn't return from her "long vacation." I also know that this has the potential to cause such confusion in her mind later on with part of her KNOWING that Jessica is no longer alive and the other part of her brain BELIEVING that she is alive and somewhere CHOOSING not to be with her. I do not know how to help her to face the fact that Jessica is not coming back. Is this why she does not want to go to the cemetery? I have never pushed her to go because I know that different people grieve differently and I respect that. If her reasoning for not going is because to see Jessica's grave would MAKE her know that she is no longer alive then maybe I SHOULD push her to go. I don't want to see Ericka hurt but I KNOW that it is far better for her to hurt and grieve now than to allow her to have this false hope and deal with what comes later. I just don't know what to do. I have been worried about Dalton because he has had such trouble talking about his feelings and I didn't want him to bottle it up until he exploded from the pressure of it all. But now I find that although Ericka has been talking about Jessica and I THOUGHT this meant she was dealing with things it really only meant that she had convinced herself that things would be ok and Jessica would be back sometime. God PLEASE guide me as to what to do to help her with this. PLEASE show me how I am supposed to be there for my children through dealing with the loss of their sister. I am soo lost when it comes to what to do here. As I was thinking these things I felt soo confused. I didn't really even know what to ask God for, how am I supposed to pray for something when I don't know what to pray for? Suddenly I remembered something I had read: "Likewise the Spirit also helpeth our infirmities: for we know not what we should pray for as we ought; but the Spirit itself maketh intercession for us with groaning which cannot be uttered." Romans 8:26 I know that God will guide me and this gives me some peace.

February 17, 2012 Today was a test for me. My Great Aunt, my Dad's Mom's sister passed away on Valentine's Day and today was her funeral. I wanted to be there for my Dad and the rest of the family, I KNEW how much it meant to me to know that when I lost Jessica my family, even those I had not seen in a long while, came to be with me. I knew though, that this would be extremely hard for me to attend a funeral this soon after Jessica's. I was determined to do it though and I

PRAYED that God would see me through. I knew that Matthew 7:7 said "Ask, and it shall be given you; seek, and ye shall find; knock, and it shall be opened unto you." I CERTAINLY needed God to give me the strength to make it through the day. The family dinner was hard because there were so many people in such a small space, I found myself feeling faint and a bit "edgy" and had to make my way outside. Things that should not have been a reminder of Jessica AT ALL seemed to bring thoughts of her pouring into my mind. The food, the family, the laughter, all of it was a reminder that just a few shorts weeks ago I had been at another funeral for my sweet daughter, Jessica. People asked how I was doing but I could not bring myself to be honest with them. This was not the time or place for me to break down over Jessica when we were there for Hazel. So I plastered the closest thing I could get to a smile on my face and answered the words "I am here" which seemed to send each person who asked me how I was quickly away. What did they expect my answer to be? I WANTED to be able to say "I am fine" but this seemed soo much like a slap in the face to Jessica to be "fine" only a little over 5 weeks after her death and besides, I would have been LYING and this wasn't something I wanted to go around doing either. Finally the time for the funeral was there and I felt my heart almost stop in my chest as I walked down the aisle to the pew where they had us sit. As I sat I turned toward Erick only to find that he was not there. The church was so full that there were not enough seats for everyone to sit and he had stayed back at the back of the church standing. I felt panic try to take over. I NEEDED Erick with me. I had TOLD him I could not do this by myself! I went to bolt and run to him but found that my legs would not stand. I was TRAPPED in the pew with no way out and I felt like there was NO WAY I would make it through this. I had to focus on something. I had to get a hold of myself. I looked to the flowers to try and take my mind from the pain that was gripping me so tightly only to find that the arrangements were FULL of purple flowers. That was JESSICA's favorite color. SHE had purple flowers at her funeral. This could NOT be happening! I felt a hand on me; it was my Mom "Are you ok?" Somehow I found my voice and said "yes", ok so I WAS lying. WONDERFUL, I was inside a church and I was LYING. I would be lucky if I made it out of there without lightening striking me. I know that Hazel was a wonderful woman, minister, teacher, and servant of God. I knew this BEFORE I went to her funeral and I SOMETIMES managed to hear these words coming out of the mouth of the preachers who were preaching the sermon but for the most part I was feeling saddened by the fact that Hazel had soo many years to do God's work and to live her life and Jessica had only 18 years! I hope that God and Hazel understand my only being able to half mourn for Hazel today. I hope that they understand that I did not mean any disrespect to a woman who so OBVIOUSLY deserved it. As we walked past the casket and I looked down I did not so much see Hazel as I did the purple outfit she was wearing and the handkerchief with purple on it that she had in her hand. One thought crossed my mind before I felt myself begin to give way to tears and become shaky "Take care of my Jessica for me Hazel. PLEASE take care of her for me and let her know how much she is loved." I could not make it out of the church quick enough. I had to find Erick. I had to be in his arms before I lost it completely. I found him outside and cried as he held me. I could not go to the graveside service. I could not watch as someone else so dear to our family was about to be lowered into the ground. I needed to distance myself from the funeral that was being officiated by the same funeral home as Jessica's. No longer did the sight of my childhood friend Joe give me any type of happy feelings from remembering memories from our childhood. All I could think of when I looked at him today was "You were there to see my baby after she died. You were there with her when I could not be. You were there when they lowered her body into the ground." I am glad that there was someone I knew and trust to do those things but it did not make things any easier on me on this day. Mom assured me that people would understand when I told her that I was going to my brother's house rather than go to the graveside service. I hate to say that at that point I did not care if they understood or not. I KNEW that if I went I might not make it out of there without being carried out and I could not do that to myself or Hazel's family. My family was wonderful never saying anything to me about not being able to make it through it or questioning me in any way. Mom, Dad, Kevin, Sharyne, Chase, Allison, one of Chase' friends, Erick and I all went out to eat dinner later that night and enjoyed each other's company. I am thankful for such a wonderful family that takes me as I am and doesn't push me to do more than I am able. I know that there are many out there who do not have this luxury and I feel sorry for them. Without my family and God I would not be where I am today in respect to Jessica's death. I am far from healed. My life is FAR from "normal" but I am living as best as I can.

February 18, 2012 The farther I get into this Blog the more evident it becomes that God is using me to try and help bring peace to those who are mourning the loss of a loved one. In doing so though, others are also helping to bring peace to me. I received a letter from my second cousin who had lost her daughter back in 1995. Her daughter was a school teacher and a mother of 3 boys ages 8, 6, and 3 years old. She shared with me some of the things that occurred after her daughter's death that were unable to be explained but that gave comfort. The first thing she shared with me was that the morning after the accident her high school students were so grieved and one boy went up and sat down at her desk. Her daughter always turned her calendar to the next day when she left at the end of the day. The student could not believe what the note that he read on the calendar. This was the note: "The goal of teaching is to enable those taught to get along without the teacher." The week after the funeral she and her husband had gone back home with her daughter's husband to help him with the boys and finalize things that had to be taken care of from the wreck. That week she was in their bedroom and she found three little cars that her daughter had bought to someday give to her three sons. This is what was written on them:

Love Note to My Son

Dear Son,

God gave to me

My greatest joy

When I heard the words

You have a "boy"

You are in my every thought

My prayers are sent to you

Asking for God's wisdom

In all you attempt to do.

Asking for God's Guidance

To send along your way

And for His courage

To face life day by day.

Always strive

In whatever you want to do

For with God's help

He will see you through.

Wow, what amazing signs from God. She also told me of how the holidays would be difficult for my family as they were for hers and explained that the first Christmas after their daughter's death she and her husband had spent alone. She said she was reading in the music room of her house when she heard a most terrible crash in the house. She jumped up and found that their big mirror in the bathroom had just fallen off the wall. She said they could not imagine why when there was no one else around. She was talking to a friend on the phone after that and her friend said to her "I believe the message is that your lives have been shattered, but you've got to pick up the pieces and go on." I am thankful for her sharing this with me. I know that she has survived the loss of her daughter and this gives me strength to carry on and survive myself. You see, not only did she lose her daughter but then, in 2003 she lost her 19 year old grandson. She also shared scriptures with me and one of the scriptures she shared was 2 Corinthians 1:3-5 "Blessed *be* God, even the Father of our Lord Je'-sus Christ, the Father of mercies, and the God of all comfort; Who comforteth us in all our tribulation, that we may be able to comfort them which are in any trouble, by the comfort wherewith we ourselves are comforted of God. For as the sufferings of Christ abound in us, so our consolation also aboundeth by Christ." Again, I felt God urging me to use my situation and how I was surviving it to help others.

I have reached out to others who I know have lost a child. I was afraid to do so, afraid that I would make them angry or that they would not want my help. I felt God's urging me to reach out though and so I did. I am so glad that I did because I can FEEL that this person needs me and I believe that I need her as well. We both are mothers who lost a daughter at a very young age and we KNOW how the hurt is so all consuming. We may not know EXACTLY how the other feels because each person handles and feels things differently but we have an understanding of the deep sense of loss and the pain that will never go away. I WISH that she and I could have become friends under different circumstances; I wish that it was not the loss of our daughters that is bringing us together. We cannot turn back time no matter how much we wish we could though so I will make of it what I can.

I wish that I could say that today was good. I thought it was going to be but then my nerve issues kicked in and everything went south. I didn't take the medication for the tingling in my limbs last night because the Dr. said I did not have to take them unless I was having the symptoms but I COULD. I always feel like I take more medication than I should anyway so I wanted to only take the meds when I was feeling the need to take them. Well, last night went well but then today, around 3pm the tingling set in and this time it was worse than it had ever been. It felt as if the bottom of my feet were on FIRE, like they were being burned from the inside out. If you looked at the bottom of my feet you could see the red shiny spots that even LOOKED as if those areas were being burned. I was determined to tough it out because the medication for it makes me sleepy which is why I was directed to take it at night. After about an hour though, I could FEEL that the on edge of my nerves was becoming more than I could take. I was jittery and anxious and I NEEDED to get this to stop before I went into a full blown anxiety attack. I told Erick what was going on and asked his opinion about taking it now rather than tonight and he agreed that he thought it was best for me to take it now. Of course my taking the medication ended up with me sleeping until 8pm but it did take care of the nerve issues and when I woke up I was calm again. I HATE feeling out of control like this! I HATE that most of the time I really would rather just spend my time in bed than deal with anything that life has to throw at me. I have the will to work on the blog at least once a day usually but other than that I have no will for much at all. I have the will to help others not feel what I am feeling which is what keeps me going with it and with helping others but that seems to be where my will stops. Don't get me wrong, I am not suicidal or anything like that. I just feel that my purpose in life is to help others and in the meantime I just go through the motions of life. Some of those motions seem important to me and so I do them and others just seem like they don't need to be done. It is as if I am in a fog and the fog is soo heavy that it takes all my strength to do just a few things. I pick daily what of the things I have to do seem the most important and those I do but the other things I simply don't worry about. I look at Erick and the kids who are going on with things in their lives and I just feel stuck. I have not been able to do what they do for some while but now I feel almost USELESS in the rolls of our everyday lives. I forget to pick things up from town, to make phone calls, to lay out things for supper. The list goes on and on. I always remember to say I Love You when I talk to someone and to tell people to be careful when they are driving and ask them to let me know when they get home safely. These are things that are EMBEDED into my mind now. NEVER forget to say I Love You because you just never know if that might have been your last chance. I always have that uneasy feeling when my kids or Erick can't be located because it has been brought front and center into my mind that I have NO CONTROL over what happens in life. The other stuff just isn't important enough for my mind to focus on and I wonder how long my family will stay understanding of this. I wonder when they will get tired of my brooding and expect me to pick up and go on. A card came to me from the same cousin and in it was this verse: "I have loved you with an everlasting love." This was from Jeremiah 31:3. God PLEASE teach my family about this everlasting love so that they will be here with me and for me and be understanding of what I am going through when they cannot understand it themselves. Give me the strength to carry on and to become stronger each day as you promised Isaiah 41:10 "Fear though not; for I *am* with thee: be not dismayed; for I *am* thy God: I will strengthen thee; yea, I will help thee; yea, I will uphold thee with the right hand of my rightousness."

This picture was taken by a fellow mother who also lost her daughter. This was actually taken when there was a storm brewing. The first time I looked at this photo was after Jessica's death though and I did not see a brewing storm. What I saw was heavens bright light shining down through the doom. I could almost FEEL the excitement of heaven beginning to open up as I gazed at it. The black and white picture does not do it justice but I hope that you can still FEEL the hope that this picture brought to me.

Thanks Kellie Davis for allowing me to use one of your photos in my book. You have an AMAZING talent.

Afterward

My struggle with dealing with the loss of my precious child, Jessica Power, has far from ended. I know the loss of her is something that I will feel for my entire life. I feel the need to stop this book here though so that I can get it out in order to be able to help those people that God has called me to help. I do not know WHY February 18, 2012 is the last day that God has guided me to write about in this book. When I first started to think about where I would end it I felt it should be some milestone like an anniversary of her death or something. God however, did not lead me to end with that and in this I will follow his lead.

If you have read this book because you are grieving for the loss of a child, spouse, sibling, grandchild, or any other family member I urge you to remember that everyone grieves differently. Do not let ANYONE tell you that how you are grieving or what you are feeling is wrong. (Unless of course it is hurting yourself or someone else physically.) There is no timeline for grief; there are no RULES that say that grieving stops at a certain amount of time after death or that it ever stops at all. Do what YOU need to do to survive. Seek guidance from God and he WILL help you through it. Do NOT be afraid to go to him because you are angry with him or mad at him. He KNOWS how you feel and he is OK with it. God KNOWS we are human and he loves us just the same.

If you have read this book because you are family, or friends of someone who has lost a loved one the number one thing I say to you is BE PATIENT. Do not try and put a time on when they should “snap out of it”. BE there for them. Do NOT tell them to call if they need something, they won’t. They do not want to be a burden to you and when they need you they most likely do not have the strength or the will to make that call. Do not forget them AFTER the funeral; this will be the hardest time for them. For the outside world the loved one has been laid to rest and healing will begin but for their loved ones they are now WITHOUT them and without the comfort that comes from everyone directly following a death. The MOST IMPORTANT thing I can tell you is let them talk about their feelings. Whether their feelings are of grief, pain, anger, resentment, or just plain rubbish they NEED to have someone they can talk to. DON’T take things personally if they become quick to anger or hurt. Every nerve ending in their body feels like it is on edge and this WILL come out at those that they Love the most.

PLEASE feel free to email me with questions or information about my book. I am eager to hear what you have to say. If you need someone to listen to who will not judge you I am here as well. frommyhearttogod@live.com

www.ingramcontent.com/pod-product-compliance
Ingram Content Group UK Ltd.
Pitfield, Milton Keynes, MK11 3LW, UK
UKHW051136260726
13967UKWH00010B/3092